MW01254835

50 VEGETARIAN RECIPES
from 50 Years at
CLAIRE'S CORNER COPIA

50 VEGETARIAN RECIPES
from 50 Years at
CLAIRE'S CORNER COPIA

CLAIRE CRISCUOLO, RN

Globe
Pequot

Essex, Connecticut

Globe Pequot

An imprint of The Globe Pequot Publishing Group, Inc.
64 South Main Street
Essex, CT 06426
www.globepequot.com

Distributed by NATIONAL BOOK NETWORK

Copyright © 2025 Claire Criscuolo
Photos by Lisa Nichols

All rights reserved. No part of this book may be reproduced in any form or by any electronic or mechanical means, including information storage and retrieval systems, without written permission from the publisher, except by a reviewer who may quote passages in a review.

British Library Cataloguing in Publication Information available

Library of Congress Cataloging-in-Publication Data

Names: Criscuolo, Claire, author.
Title: 50 vegetarian recipes from 50 years at Claire's Corner Copia /
  Claire Criscuolo.
Description: Essex, Connecticut : Globe Pequot, [2025] | Includes index.
Identifiers: LCCN 2024042484 (print) | LCCN 2024042485 (ebook) | ISBN
  9781493089055 (paperback) | ISBN 9781493089062 (ebook)
Subjects: LCSH: Claire's Corner Copia (Restaurant) | Vegetarian cooking. |
  LCGFT: Cookbooks.
Classification: LCC TX837 .C77225 2025 (print) | LCC TX837 (ebook) | DDC
  641.5/636—dc23/eng/20241029
LC record available at https://lccn.loc.gov/2024042484
LC ebook record available at https://lccn.loc.gov/2024042485

♾️™ The paper used in this publication meets the minimum requirements of American National Standard for Information Sciences—Permanence of Paper for Printed Library Materials, ANSI/NISO Z39.48-1992.

The author and The Globe Pequot Publishing Group, Inc., assume no liability for accidents happening to, or injuries sustained by, readers who engage in the activities described in this book.

This book is dedicated with so much love and gratitude to every single person who came through our doors for the past fifty years! You made this sweet little place of ours a blessing! Thank you.

Peace,
Claire

contents

introduction

I grew up on Wooster Street in New Haven, Connecticut, an Italian enclave of families from Italy, mainly Amalfi. My parents, my brother Billy, and I lived with my grandparents, Assunta and Paolo Bigio, along with my mother's brother, Uncle Jim, and his wife, Aunt Rose, and their two daughters, Lois and Suzanne, in a large house with three apartments. My twin brothers, Jimmy and Paul, didn't arrive until after we moved to East Haven when I was five years old. My grandfather owned and operated Paulo Bigio and Sons, a market on the ground level of our building. I can still remember the barrels of beans and grains. There was delicious and homemade food in each apartment, and I was, as my mother often said, "a good eater!" Mornings started with my grandmother, my anonna, and warmed milk with a drop of espresso (because I was "a big girl!") and crostini with butter or apricot jam—still a favorite of mine. Lunches and suppers always included fresh soups or sauces with pastas and bountiful salads of vegetables and beans. Fruits and vegetables always dominated our meals. These foods remain a hallmark of my diet.

When we moved to East Haven my mother told us, "We're going to be Americans!" I learned this meant that we'd be living in a neighborhood with people from places other than Italy and that we needed to speak English. Later in college I read a copy of *Psychology Today* with the cover story "Food Fears." The article talked about social workers coming to the homes of newly arrived immigrants from Italy. When the social workers saw that people were eating traditional Italian foods and speaking Italian, they told the families that their children wouldn't succeed unless they assimilated. I imagine that word spread to my mother, and like every mother, she wanted her children to succeed. Still, Italian food dominated the kitchen at our house, although there was an occasional Hungarian goulash at our table. The recipe was shared by a neighbor, Mrs. Funk, but somehow it always tasted Italian—I'm thinking my mother added basil!

Although my mother worked as a housekeeper, she was home each day when we came home from school. And she was always there with a few homemade Italian cookies, a glass of milk or lemonade during the summer, and some sliced apples or other fruit (yes, she sliced the fruits for us—I was totally spoiled!). My earliest memories are filled with food, because food was and is central to my happy life.

My mother's examples have always guided me. We were poor when I was a girl; my father was injured in the navy and spent much of his time in the VA hospital. My mother cleaned houses for a living, so money was always tight, but real food was always a priority. She couldn't spoil us with "things," but she absolutely spoiled us with food. She made fresh soups and sauces, dressings and desserts, bread and pizza dough. Even fresh lemonade all summer. She had a summer garden to supply tomatoes, eggplants, peppers, and herbs. We even had an Italian plum tree on our front lawn—really! And family and friends always brought my mom vegetables from their gardens, so summers were filled with freshness. During the off season, we had a lot of onions and carrots, but in season vegetables, beans, pastas, and grains dominated our meals.

Everything was made fresh, and nothing was ever wasted. An early lesson I still think about happened when one night, as I was clearing the table after dinner, my mother saw me heading to the trash pail with a piece of lettuce left over from our dinner salad. She said, "Why are you throwing that away?" I asked, "You want me to save a piece of lettuce?" Her answer—"You want to waste it?" Lesson learned. My mother used

cloth towels instead of paper towels and covered a dish of leftovers with a plate—she never even owned paper towels or plastic wrap until I graduated from college. There were no trash bags either: We filled the plastic trash pail in our kitchen and emptied it into the big trash barrel outside—each night. Then we would wash our kitchen trash pail and start again. I think that if we really want to be eco-friendly, we'd revert back to that system, but we are spoiled by conveniences. At Claire's Corner Copia we try to do our part by recycling everything we can. Thankfully, our landlord, Yale Properties, allows us the infrastructure to compost our kitchen scraps. It's a start!

I know that my early exposure to real food has and always will guide my choices for myself and for Claire's Corner Copia. And it's why I want everyone to experience real food, made fresh, using really good, organic ingredients. Freshly made food will always taste better than something that was made weeks or months ago and stored on a shelf—we just need to know the difference, and eating real food will assure that we will always know the difference. It matters because we all matter!

I had the privilege of standing alongside my mother as she cooked and baked, assisting with the rolling of meatballs, mixing the cream puff batters, stirring the soups and sauces. Watching, listening, smelling, and tasting!

During my high school years, my brother Billy began to spend his summers

traveling throughout Europe. During the school year, after school, he worked in a factory to save for his summer trips. He'd come home from his travels with stories of the foods he had eaten and the people he had met. This led me to the East Haven Library and right to the cookbook section. On trips to New York City, I'd visit museums with Billy, and there was always a lunch or dinner in an "exotic" restaurant: French, Chinese, Mediterranean. At first, my mother would ask, "Don't you want to make Grandma's foods?" I'd always reply, "I do, but I also want to make other people's grandmothers' foods." And this is what we do, every day, at Claire's Corner Copia. I hope that one day, as we're eating together, we'll realize that we all want the same things: happiness, good health, and peace, for ourselves and for our children.

Opening Claire's Corner Copia on September 17, 1975!

In 1973, when Frank and I first met, he was a musician, twenty-six, and about to leave for Florida where he planned to play solo acts in hotels. I was twenty-three and a nursing student. Well, his plans changed! We were so in love that we were married a year and a half after we met. And our love affair blossomed to include working together in what was to be Claire's Corner Copia. Yes, a love affair, with all the people and all the food that made and continue to make this journey a blessing.

When we think of a restaurant, we often think it's all about the food. Well, I can say, and I do say this over and over again, "It's the people!" The people bring the joy, grow and deliver and prepare the food, and support this crazy but wonderful adventure we call Claire's Corner Copia.

It wasn't and never will be a totally easy ride—again, words from my mom, "If it was easy, it likely wouldn't be worth all the work." Of course, there were the proverbial bumps: the broken air conditioners (always during the hottest periods) or the late deliveries (crazy how time made me realize that not having peppers for one day wasn't the end of the world, and ditto for not having soup ready at 11:30), but honestly, there aren't many things I'd change—all were lessons learned.

Frank and I were newly married, and he was driving a truck at the time because he didn't believe that playing music in clubs late at night was a good idea for our lives together. I was a psychiatric nurse. But we wanted to be together, so much so that we wanted to work together. I suggested we open a restaurant. Every summer since we dated, we had visited Frank's childhood vacation spot, where his family lived when they first arrived from Naples, Italy. Gloucester, Massachusetts, was that place. It was a fishing town where Frank's family owned a trucking company that trucked fish to the Fulton Fish Market. Frank and I always visited each summer, for a day or for a few days, and there were a lot of restaurants, but one was my favorite—The Raven! They had a blackboard menu each day with a few specials. I thought we could open a restaurant like that and I could spend my days cooking. Well, that's not exactly what happened. It turns out there is an enormous amount of work, outside the kitchen, that happens every single day. And I love every aspect. Especially the people—inside and outside the kitchen. All right, I'm not in love with the administrative parts where I don't spend time with my restaurant family, but it must be done. Thankfully, our office manager and all-around incredible woman Bobbi Dunne makes it easy—and she makes us better because she really thinks like Frank!

There are so many people to thank for our success. My brothers and Frank were still banging nails into the cabinets on the very morning we opened. My sister-in-law Kathy often helped out in the restaurant on what I referred to as "Friends and Family Day" when we were short-staffed, and she's always the first one I call to help me edit my words on paper. Now my niece and godchild Carley has joined the editing team for me.

My brothers remain a presence with their advice about repairs and finances, along with my nephew Branden and his wife Laura, who offer marketing advice. My mother- and father-in-law remained a presence for many years, which was so much help for us because my mother-in-law was an amazing cook. Years ago, it was said that men might say, "I married

her because she can cook." I always say, "I married Frank because his mother could cook!" She embraced my vegetarian diet and made delicious foods for me, and several of these dishes remain on our specials menu at Claire's Corner Copia—dishes like Stuffed Peppers, Lasagne Rolls, Escarole e Fagioli, and more.

"It always works out" is a motto here at Claire's, although one of our fabulous managers, Ashley Suraci, rephrased it to, "*We* always make it work." That little rearrangement of words puts us in the driver's seat to *make* it work.

Our organic farmers and other vendors are critical to our success—without good ingredients, there could be no Claire's Corner Copia.

Back in our very early days, when the gates at Yale University were closed off to the city, students would climb the fence and come to us, and honestly, it was those early supporters who allowed us to continue to grow.

Money was so tight back then because we were so different—no meat, no smoking—and at first, customers were few, limited mainly to the Yale students and some others. There were times when we nearly went out of business.

Everyone Can Use a Little Help along the Way

Our early years at Claire's Corner Copia were difficult. Gates at Yale University were

locked, preventing many students from wandering off campus. Thankfully, there were some who actually climbed the fence to venture out and to eat at our place. And students like Terry Hawkins wrote about us and our smoothies in the *Yale Daily News*. Word got around and slowly we balanced the books to keep us in business.

We began by buying the Carmel Corn Shop from the late Fred DeLuca, founder of the Subway chain. He sublet the shop to us with the intention that he'd open a Subway there when the timing was right. Our intention was to open a restaurant that served homemade foods, made from scratch using fresh ingredients. We would serve foods from our moms' kitchens and foods that I read about or learned of from Billy's travels. We had little money to make all the changes immediately, but we managed. First, we had a contest to name the place. Jeff Hall, an undergraduate at Yale University, wrote "Claire's Corner Copia." We thought this play on words was perfect! But the giant, white plastic sign above the shop read "Carmel Corn Shop" and had a giant Coca-Cola logo on it. I called Coca-Cola headquarters and asked if they would change the name for us. They told me they no longer paid for signage changes. So I suggested they make an exception because we were advertising their product on what we believe is the best corner in the city and if they couldn't change it, we'd be forced to try another company, like maybe . . . Pepsi! The sign was changed.

Next, I sold the huge copper bowl used to make caramel corn—I still regret having to do that because it was stunningly beautiful and would have made a gorgeous planter for our corner! But that sale gave us the funds to buy a four-burner household stove with an oven. After that I removed the light from the stainless-steel warming bed for the freshly made caramel corn and turned it into a salad bar. I needed an ice machine, so I partnered with a soda company that provided us with an ice dispenser along with their soda dispenser. An ice cream vendor came by and said that if we sold ice cream, they'd give us the display case and a freezer. We needed a freezer to store the pita bread we planned to use. We planned for Frank to drive to New Jersey each week to buy fresh, hot-off-the-bakery-line pita bread from Toufayan Bakery! We knew that freezing the pita while still warm would make for the best pita to serve each day. We'd just take out a few bags each morning. We were both newly in business and they were wonderful partners with us. I can still remember the smell of warm pita bread that permeated Frank's car! Frank would always bring me a special treat, like spanakopita, also made at Toufayan. We continue to serve Toufayan whole wheat pita bread today, nearly fifty years later!

Before long, it was time to open—September 17, 1975. And it was time for me to ask my mom what soup should be the first one I made—vegetable bean with barley, she said. "It's so healthy and everyone likes

it." And there we began! Signs were painted on boards, with a list of pita bread sandwiches and falafel sandwiches, like the ones I ate during visits to New York City with my brother Billy. Even chicken appeared on the menu in 1975. Our blackboard specials included chicken kiev, or souvlaki, again with a nod to our America, where we always want everyone to have a seat at the table!

The owner of the lease never imagined that we would survive, but we did. But not without help from strangers whom I always thought of as angels.

My favorite "angel" is Mr. Goodman, our dairy vendor who saved me. Mr. Goodman provided us with the butter and sour cream for our desserts and the cheeses for our sandwiches. I was sobbing one day when he came to deliver, and he was so kind. I explained that we didn't have a lot of business and I was out of money, and even my husband thought we should close and I should return to work as a nurse. Mr. Goodman immediately said, "Don't pay me! Use the money for your rent, because I know when spring arrives and the weather is better, people will come. Your food is good!" He was right. Many years later, a customer, Rebecca, came in and said, "You probably won't remember my father," and somehow I knew. I asked if Mr. Goodman was her father and she was shocked by my response. Rebecca and now her daughter, Avery, are faithful and wonderful customers in our Claire's Family! #itsthepeople

Years have passed and our business has continued to grow. Shortly after we opened, Joel Schiavone bought the building where we held our corner space. He wanted a T-shirt shop on the corner, so he took back the corner, and our restaurant wrapped around the corner shop. We bought the jewelry shop several years later, when Mr. Hazian wanted to retire. Shortly after that, Mamma's Pizza wanted to move and we expanded into that location. I promised myself that we would never expand again, because it's just too much work! Then, once we were totally used to our space, Yale Properties called and asked if I wanted to reannex our original corner, where the T-shirt shop had been. I was cleaning the dining room when I got that call and said, "Sure, that sounds good." Then the pandemic hit. Timing really is everything. We desperately needed a new kitchen floor—it was literally held together with cardboard and duct tape! We may have skimped on our renovations, but we never skimped on our ingredients and our fair wages to our beloved staff. No regrets! The renovation didn't exactly go as planned, but neither did the pandemic, so we took advantage of the time and renovated everything. Thank God for federally funded programs. We had level floors for the first time ever! And gorgeous quartz countertops. During the renovation, we were concerned that it wouldn't feel the same, but the reality is that it's the people who fill Claire's Corner Copia—and my heart. Always has, and still does, thanks to our team! I am so blessed to continue to have our first managers as my dear friends. Sara Sylvester (Hernandez); Rose Naclerio (Albin) (Rose actually met her husband, Tom, at Claire's—he managed on evenings and Rose on days); Donna Nuzello; Geri Mauhs; Kirsten Kvist-Hansen (on an exchange program from Denmark); Mary-Ellen Eisses; Don Jackson; and Erin Guild managed during earlier days as we were growing.

For more than a decade, Juana Lopez, Margie Cancel, Rosie Hernandez (my Mini-Me), Tonny Morales, Tia Dozier, Ashley Suraci, and Adriana Garcia have managed our sweet little place, our kitchen and bakery, and have kept us committed to excellence through their hard work and delicious food—including all the laughs that really get us through the busiest days. Gerardo Meneses, Celestino Romano, Adriana Garcia, Feliz Cabrera, Patti Portillo, Elfemia, RK, Luke, Thien, Isabel, Johanna, and the many, many people who work in our Claire's Family make us better.

Our business really took off around 1994, when my first cookbook, *Claire's Corner Copia Cookbook*, was published. This was perfect timing, as science continued to prove that eating well matters! We always try to educate, and we continue to post signs about heart health, mental health, and general well-being and how a healthy diet relates to better health. Thankfully, science continues to prove that we can affect our health through our lifestyles, food, exercise, and community. A cookbook from a little restaurant in New Haven turned out to be a big deal. We had hundreds of people come out for our first book signing. I negotiated with the bookstores and agreed to have the first signing be at the store that would donate the greatest percentage to the charity of my choice—Aids Project New Haven.

Following the release of the book, I've been privileged to tour the country and teach cooking classes, as well as lead small cooking demonstrations on local and national television stations and sit for interviews on radio stations. It was eye-opening to hear from people in other parts of our country who were also interested in eating well. Thank you to all the schools who invited me to teach classes and meet the wonderful people who make this amazing country of ours so special. Those were exciting times and I loved meeting the people who wanted to eat healthier. I especially loved the Midwest. Why not? That's where most of the soybeans are grown! It was exhausting—television demos, bookstore events with more demos, classes, and repeat. But my Frank came with me to all the earlier events, which made it even more fun. We'd spend an extra day or two in each city to explore and to meet the wonderful people. Once again, it was the people who made it so special. Cooking school students would often bring me gifts, like a bag of soybeans or a special salt, and share their stories about their journey to better health through better eating.

One story that stuck out was from a woman in the Midwest who didn't have

access to romaine lettuce—this was back in the mid-1990s when iceberg was the only thing. She was so clever to ask friends and neighbors if they'd share a case of romaine with her—and they wanted to—so she approached the produce manager at her local grocery store and he agreed to bring in a case if they would buy it. Problem solved! Another clever lady who lived alone found it challenging to make a pot of soup for one. Again, she gathered friends and neighbors and asked if they wanted to start a soup exchange—turns out that concept works beyond Christmas cookies. Problem solved! I loved how people shared their stories and that the book I wrote helped them to eat more fruits, vegetables, and beans and less meat. I truly found my purpose!

I owe a huge debt of thanks to everyone at Yale University and Yale Properties. The students and faculty are the lifeblood of our place! Without their support and the support of our loving community, we could never be the success we are, and we'd never be able to afford to pay our beloved Claire's Family fair wages or to keep our sweet little place in good condition (that is a huge and ongoing task), and we'd never be able to support our community in the many ways we do, from sponsorships to coat and hygiene drives, donations, and volunteer work.

Special shout out to local jazz and swing group Proof of the Pudding, and to Sandra Cashion, who always sends us love through performances and visits.

People always comment on "the vibe, the energy" of our sweet little place. Once again, it's the people! Our customers help others—it's as simple as that. New Haven is home to many nonprofits and volunteers who tutor or mentor children; work to prevent homelessness, protect animals, and protect our environment; offer scholarships; help the elderly and children who are sick; educate our children and adults—really, we have helpers who work so hard to make life better for all who can use a hand up. These are friends who manage New Haven Reads, All Our Kin, Clifford Beers Clinic, Saint Martin de Porres School, Connecticut CASA, Marrakech, Ronald McDonald House Charities, and so many more. Many of them meet at Claire's Corner Copia, and I really think that's where the wonderful energy comes from—really, it's love! Love for each other, love for a better world. It is a privilege to be here in this city where people care for each other in many ways that lift others.

Both our hashtag and our motto are painted on the soffits in our dining room, surrounded by paintings of farms, reminders of what matters. #BeKinderThanNecessary is also printed on our mugs, T-shirts, and paper goods, because we all need that reminder.

Our motto is, "The only compelling reason we have been given more love than we need, more food than we need, and more resources than we need is so that we may

Be Kinder Than Necessary

Dear Claire,

Today was my friend's birthday, and naturally we want to treat him to a slice of Claire's cake. Then we saw the sign about how someone had broken in.

Claire's has been such a source/symbol of joy/goodwill/friendship to me in my last 3½ years in N. Haven that I am devastated that anyone would try to harm it.

I would like to do anything I can to help, so if you want, I can come in tomorrow (Monday) and help by cleaning/waiting tables/anything, just so you and the rest of your awesome staff know that we appreciate (and are addicted to) the wonderful goddess that is CLAIRE'S.

Cynthia ♡

Another favorite came from another wonderful customer.

share the excess with those who have been given less!" —The God Squad.

Again, a reminder of why we are here.

For those times when we are exhausted by the troubles of the world, we read those simple yet important reminders. Those words, and the words of some of our customers who have written to us over the years, are reminders that kindness matters, and that we matter!

I want to share two of my favorite letters (I've kept them on the walls in my home office). This first one was handwritten!

Dear Claire and Team,

A love letter to Claire's Corner Copia is both so simple and so difficult to write— there is just too much love!! So I guess I'll begin with the story of the first time I found my way to Claire's. When I was a junior in high school, my mom and I traveled to New Haven to go on a college visit. After a long travel day, we walked past Claire's and it was love at first sight. We escaped the cold weather and sat down in the cozy, inviting, and welcom-

ing Claire's interior for a meal and split multiple entrees and desserts—everything was so good, we couldn't choose just one! I remember telling my mom that this vegetarian spot would be my go-to place if I ended up being lucky enough to come to college here.

Fast forward a few years later and I am now a junior in college and conveniently live right around the corner from Claire's. By absolutely no coincidence, might I add! Since moving to New Haven, Claire's has become my little piece of home. When I'm having a bad day, there's nothing a mini loaf or sun butter cookie can't fix! When I'm having a good day, there's no better place to grab a treat to celebrate!

Claire's has become the place I take all of my local friends and visiting friends. All three of my older brothers and both of my parents have now been to Claire's—all on separate visits!

And all of them love it for the same reasons I do. Claire's has so many delicious and healthy options that are all made with love. Now when my family and friends come to visit, the first stop on their New Haven checklist is always a visit to Claire's.

I love the love that Claire's has brought into my life. The carry-out park picnic with friends on sunshiny summer days, the warm meals and desserts shared with loved ones as we fill each other in on life, and the smiling, kindhearted individuals stand-

ing behind the Claire's counter who make Claire's feel like home (and who know me by both my name and my usual order!).

So, as you can see, naming just one thing that I love about Claire's is quite difficult for me. One thing I know for sure, however, is that my love for Claire's will never fade. I already know that I will be a frequent visitor to Claire's during visits to New Haven after I graduate and cannot wait to continue introducing more loved ones to my little piece of home away from home.

Love Always,
Julia Dvorak

It is a blessing and a joy to be a place where people feel the love that radiates from the space, the food, and the people who make it.

Thank you to every single person we've served or worked with along the way, from September 17, 1975, to this very special anniversary to celebrate fifty years of love in this sweet little place we call Claire's Corner Copia. My team, my Claire's Family, are the reason we can do what we do!

The Pandemic

In the fall of 2019, Yale Properties, our landlord, asked if we wanted to reannex our original space. I loved that idea, being back on our original corner! The plan was to open the wall and redo our kitchen floor around

The only compelling reason we've been given more love than we need, more food than we need, and more resources than we need, is so that we may share with others who have been given less. - "God Squad" early June 2020, right after Yale commencement and the reunions. Easy peasy!

Well, things don't always turn out as planned.

In the winter of 2020, I started hearing about a virus, a possible pandemic that would likely come to the United States. I called a friend, Adria Winfield, who at the time was teaching in China. She confirmed our fears that something powerful was growing and it wasn't good.

Like everyone else, I was worried about protecting myself and everyone I cared about. I've always been close with our health department, but from early 2020, I practically had Brian Wnek, our health inspector, on speed dial. He was so kind and always helpful and supportive. I needed to know how to protect my team, my restaurant! Of course, there wasn't much information at the time. So I also relied on social media and the work of Dr. Michael Greger and his book *How to Survive a Pandemic.* I also followed Dr. Jamie Rutland, who was offering helpful tips to survive this virus. He taught me words like "monoclonal antibodies" and so on. I ordered bleach, alcohol, and tea tree oil for disinfectant and so many gallons of hand sanitizer that we didn't run low for three years. I admit, I do tend to overreact! But this time it played in my favor. Like I imagine for most people, I was terrified that I couldn't protect myself and my community at Claire's Corner Copia. At least I had disinfectants! We had many, many meetings at Claire's to prepare for a shutdown. And we donated a lot

of food, both prepared and ingredients, when we shut down on March 16, 2020.

There was also the Gaggle. The Gaggle is a small group of my friends (an artist, a retired head of pediatric oncology, a high-end realtor, and me) who met pretty much every day at four o'clock during the pandemic for Zoom Happy Hour. Our happy hour consisted mainly of advice for me regarding the restaurant and it was invaluable, because we discussed my renovations and business and we brought in speakers who shared their expertise including nutrition, dramaturgy, and poetry. It was a terrific distraction from the pressures of the business and the perfect antidote to loneliness. Community is everything! Just ask our brilliant surgeon general, Dr. Vivek Murthy, who literally wrote the book on the importance of community—the title is *Together*!

Timing . . . Actually, it turned out to be a much bigger job for us to close for the renovation in 2020, with unexpected load-bearing walls and the fact that it's an old building—more than a hundred years old. Now that we were forced to shut down, Yale Properties stepped right in with the architects, contractors, painters, and planners. Yale Properties was a godsend! The renovation kept me busy, with nearly daily visits (and lots of face masks) to our space, as walls came down and floors and counters got ripped up and out.

Still, I worried about how I could support my team. I am forever grateful to our Connecticut lieutenant governor, Susan Bysewitz, and our congresswoman, Rosa DeLauro, who let me know about grants that kept us in business and covered expenses while we were closed, and beyond.

My team and I kept in contact through phone calls, group messages, outdoor pizza parties, and luncheons, and throughout the ordeal, I reminded them that "I cannot promise that I will have every answer we need, but I do promise that I will always do every single thing in my power to safely get us through this." We stuck together, and we lost only one team member who decided to move to South Carolina. Everyone else came back to help us rebuild.

My brother Paul knew that I needed some help in paying my team before they could get benefits, and he always came through. And to make me feel better about accepting his help, he always reminded me that he was an essential worker and was working—a lot! He's an angel.

My friends Rhoda and Peggy also offered to help with grocery money for my team who had families to feed. Thank you.

And as always, Yale came to the rescue! They assigned students from the School of Management to help us with marketing. I am so grateful to the SOM team, especially Samantha for her encouragement and guidance; she has been a loyal customer since her undergrad days.

Customers often asked if I was testing new recipes while we were shut down. No, not even one! But I did spend many days speaking with engineers to find ways to purify the air in our restaurant and to make us safer. I learned about ion generators, Merv filters, HEPA filters, and ratings to trap virus particles.

In early summer, restaurants were given the green light to reopen for takeout but not for indoor service. I didn't want to reopen until it was safe for takeout *and* dine-in, because if it wasn't safe enough for our customers, how could it be safe enough for our team?

Finally, we reopened at noon on August 21, 2020. And it was one of the happiest days for us, with many of our friends and family, customers, media, and government officials present, including a favorite of ours, Senator Richard Blumenthal, who was always a great supporter when I cochaired (with my dear friend Dotty Weston-Murphy) Cooking for CASA events to benefit children in foster care.

We were still required to keep a safe distance from others, but honestly, there was a lot of hugging! We believe that love is worth a risk.

We continued to open and close down again for another year or more. Whenever the virus struck one of us at Claire's, we would close down for about five days. We weren't taking any chances. As the years passed, the virus has thankfully died down, and we've returned to our old schedules, even though some folks who work in offices still work from their homes. I'm glad we are back together, cooking and baking, laughing, and enjoying this community of ours. Our community!

Bumps in the Road

As with everyone and everything, changes happen. Thankfully, most have been good for us: amazing people working for us, so many blessings, and so many reasons to be grateful. Still, bad things sometimes happen. Over the years, freezer doors have fallen off; dough mixer beaters have "magically" snapped in half, leaving our bakers with only giant whisks or spoons to hand mix 60-quart bowls of batter; air conditioner compressors have stopped during the hottest of summer days—and always after 4 p.m. on a Friday! All of that has happened to us.

Those things are no fun, of course, but we call those B-category tragedies, compared to the horrors that have impacted the world beyond our sweet little place. First, of course, we think of the day when our world was rocked when those planes hit the World Trade Center buildings. We realized that our sense of security was really just a false sense of security. We joined our families that make up our United States of America and we prayed and waited to see how we could return to a semblance of peace and security. I was at home watching the news the morning of the tragedy and I immediately called the restaurant. At first, I thought we should close and go home for a while, just to be on the safe side in case the bombings continued. My manager at the time, a terrific gal, MaryEllen Eisses, here from Nova Scotia through an exchange program, thought closing was not a good idea. "The place is filled with kids from Yale, and they are crying and upset. We need to stay here for them." And we did. As they always have for us. We still look out for each other. That's what a community does! Thankfully, with time and love, our sense of security and our daily lives somehow returned to a normal, but a different normal, one where we realized more that things can change for the good and for the bad. I guess it's always been that way, but for us it was a new normal. Yet life and business returned.

My personal world and our world at Claire's Corner Copia and beyond continued to change through the years, with major events that shook us, but we always managed to get back up because of the support we have inside and outside of our sweet little place. After an accident, my beloved mother, Anna, died on March 2, 2011, which left a huge hole in my heart—she was the kindest and wisest woman I've ever known. And the first person to love me!

My personal world crashed again on December 14, 2011, when my husband, Frank, died of a cerebral aneurism— "sudden and catastrophic" was how the ER doctor explained it to me. Anyone who has lived through such a sudden loss knows that it is devastating. And anyone who

gets to live through such a loss knows that we do this because of the incredible love and support that we call family and community. I am blessed and eternally grateful to my family at home and at Claire's Corner Copia because the support and love I received, and still receive today, makes me strong and grateful. Visits, letters and cards, prayer blankets, and so much love came and rescued me. I am forever grateful for each of them, and for the reminder that it is through love and community that we find our way back to happiness.

Thank you to every single one of you who helped us get to this incredible time when we get to celebrate fifty years of love, good food, and community. I feel confident that our leaders at Claire's Corner Copia will continue our mission to build a community founded on love.

Thank you to Globe Pequot and to David Legere for believing in this book, to Mary Wheelehan for making the editing a joy (she's a vegetarian you know), to all the many people who work to make a book (it takes so many to do that), and to Lisa Nichols, the best photographer I've ever known, who brought so much beauty to life through her photos—way more than she signed up for! Thank you, Lisa, for sharing your incredible gifts and for your incredible kindness.

And above all, I give praise to God.

Love,
Claire

breakfast

Out of the horrific pandemic came a silver lining or two. After the pandemic, we saw people actually taking the time to eat breakfast. We've always known that it's important to fuel your body after the long absence from food and drink while you were sleeping. But we also knew that many people skipped breakfast because they were in a rush to get to work. That pressure to hurry has changed dramatically. We've welcomed in so many people who are looking for less stress and more self-care time. And they are eating breakfast! We have our regulars who come in alone each morning, computer in hand, and enjoy a leisurely breakfast while either working on projects or just answering emails—or even watching a movie. We also have our regulars who come in for breakfast with friends or spouses, and coworkers or classmates who have meetings over breakfast, enjoying the time to get to know the people they spend time with every day—you'd be surprised how much your spouse will say during breakfast.

But the atmosphere is much more laid back than the old, pre-pandemic meetings. Customers are enjoying a meal while conducting business—in a less stressed way than when in the office. On weekends, we're pretty packed with friends and young families who come in for breakfast or brunch, depending on the time of day. Meeting for breakfast has become the new after-work drinks. At least it has at our place. We love that!

Avocado Confetti Tartine is the newest addition to our breakfast menu and it has become super popular. We think it's a lot more interesting and yummy than plain avocado toast. We prepare it on a grilled baguette, with healthy, lycopene-rich, beautiful, halved organic heirloom cherry tomatoes scattered over our guacamole, then drizzled with a delicious, vitamin C–rich Lemon Garlic Drizzle. I hope you'll try it.

And I hope you'll make the time to enjoy one of our breakfast recipes and start the day with a good plate of self-care.

To my sweet darlings,

Do you know how much you are loved? All the way around the world forever and a day. And how do you suppose out of all the little darlings in the world we got the very best ones? Be good and take care of each other. We know you will do great things in the world.

Yours always,
XOXO

Huevos Rancheros

Back in 1994, during a book tour to promote my first cookbook, *Claire's Corner Copia Cookbook*, I was teaching classes in Dallas, Texas. A kind cooking school director invited me for breakfast the day of my class. She told me that she was going to introduce me to Huevos Rancheros. That dish was amazing! So much so that I called my restaurant immediately following the meal to ask Javier, our first cook who was from Mexico, if he could make this dish for us at Claire's. The rest really is history because this dish has been on our menu for several decades and it just keeps becoming more popular. We offer it dairy or vegan with mashed organic tofu in place of the organic eggs; vegan mozzarella and cheddar are also available in place of the dairy cheeses we stock. As always, our customers get to choose. If you don't have a batch of homemade salsa and are in a pinch for time, use your favorite jarred, store-bought salsa. We've all been there. We serve our Huevos Rancheros with sour cream, a side of our Refried Beans (page 129), guacamole, and corn chips for dipping. Ask how many eggs each person wants and fry that number.

Serves 4

1 tablespoon extra-virgin olive oil, plus 3 tablespoons for frying the eggs

4 cups salsa, homemade or your favorite store-bought

olive oil spray

4–8 organic eggs, depending on how many each person wants, or 4 ounces organic tofu per person, broken into big pieces using a fork

salt and pepper

4 ounces shredded mozzarella and cheddar cheese, dairy or vegan

Sour cream and corn chips for serving (optional)

1. Heat 1 tablespoon olive oil in a medium pot over medium-high heat for a few seconds. Add the salsa and stir to combine. Lower the heat to low-medium and bring the salsa to a simmer until heated through, stirring frequently while you fry the eggs.

2. Heat a large skillet over medium-high heat. Spray the skillet well with olive oil spray. Add the remaining olive oil to the hot skillet and gently swirl the oil to cover the bottom. Add the eggs, one at a time, trying to leave as much space as possible in between each for easier serving. Sprinkle with salt and pepper. Reduce the heat to medium and cook the eggs until they are to your liking, about 5 minutes is how I like mine. If you prefer the yolks well cooked, cover the skillet for 1 to 2 minutes while cooking until they are set the way you prefer. If you are using tofu, add the tofu to the salsa when heating it to heat your tofu at the same time.

3. Ladle the heated salsa onto a large serving platter. Using a slotted metal spatula, transfer the fried eggs onto the salsa, trying to keep the eggs as separate as possible. Sprinkle the shredded mozzarella and cheddar evenly over the top. Serve with sour cream and a big bowl of corn chips for dipping.

Farmer's Frittata

Like every other Italian American and Catholic kid, I grew up on frittatas. They were standard fare during lent and on our meatless Fridays throughout the year. We added our Farmer's Frittata to our menu several years ago when eggs reclaimed their popularity (you know; they are out, they are in . . .). Right now they are super popular at Claire's. They are delicious and can be eaten hot or cold and are loaded with protein and vegetables. Also, there are some really good vegan egg products on the market, like Just Egg, and plenty of vegan cheeses, so it's easy to make a vegan version. As with all foods, it's important to know nutritional content along with how delicious they taste, so please read the labels!

This recipe makes enough for four to six servings, for breakfast, brunch, lunch, or dinner. Just add a bowl of a nice bean and vegetable soup or a colorful salad for a lovely dinner.

Serves 4–6

¼ cup extra-virgin olive oil

½ small red onion, cut into thin slices

2 medium organic Yukon Gold potatoes, cut in thirds lengthwise, then into ¼-inch cubes

salt and pepper

1 small organic zucchini, cut in half lengthwise, then into ¼-inch slices

1 large red or orange organic bell pepper, cut in half lengthwise, seeded, and coarsely chopped

4 large basil leaves, coarsely chopped

¼ cup water

10 organic eggs

4 ounces feta cheese, crumbled

4 ounces shredded mozzarella

olive oil spray

1. Preheat the oven to 400 degrees. Heat the oil in a large skillet over medium heat. Add the onion and potatoes. Sprinkle with salt and pepper. Cover the skillet and cook, stirring frequently, for about 5 minutes, until the potatoes are just barely tender when tested with a fork. Add the zucchini, peppers, basil leaves, and water. Sprinkle a little more salt and pepper. Stir to combine. Cover and continue cooking, stirring frequently, for about 3–5 minutes, until the vegetables are tender. Remove from the heat. Carefully, taste for seasoning.

2. In a large bowl, beat the eggs with a whisk until combined. Stir in the cooked vegetables. Stir in the feta and mozzarella cheeses. Spray a 10-inch pie pan with olive oil spray. Pour egg mixture into the prepared pie dish using a rubber spatula to scrape the bowl and smooth the mixture. Bake for about 50 minutes, until the eggs are set. Cut into wedges and serve.

French Toast

Several of my friends look forward to French Toast breakfasts on my deck during summer days. I love it, too, because it's the French toast that my mom always made for us, but today, I use a multigrain sliced bread rather than the leftover Italian bread we had growing up. I think that topping the French Toast with maple syrup–sautéed bananas and blueberries makes it extra special, and I hope you do, too. Also, I freshly grate the whole nutmeg; if you try it, you'll taste the difference. I promise!

Serves 4

4 organic eggs

½ cup soy, oat, or dairy milk

½ teaspoon cinnamon

1 teaspoon pure vanilla extract

¼ teaspoon ground nutmeg, freshly grated nutmeg if you can

¼ teaspoon ground ginger

8 slices multigrain bread

olive oil spray

5 tablespoons organic Earth Balance vegan butter spread, divided

½ cup pure maple syrup

2 bananas, peeled and sliced

1 cup fresh organic blueberries

1. In a large bowl, whisk together the eggs, milk, cinnamon, vanilla, nutmeg, and ginger.

2. Heat a large skillet over medium-low heat. Put a large platter by the stove for your cooked French Toast. Spray the skillet with olive oil spray. Add 2 tablespoons of Earth Balance to the skillet and swirl the skillet to melt the spread evenly. Moving quickly, using tongs or a fork, dip a slice of the bread into the egg mixture, coating both sides, then place it into the skillet. Continue dipping the next three slices of bread (or as many as will fit in the skillet) and arrange them single layer in the skillet. Cook for 2–3 minutes, until the underside is golden brown when using a long metal spatula to lift a slice. Using the metal spatula, turn the slices of bread and cook the other side for about 1–2 minutes, until the underside is browned. Transfer the cooked French Toast to the large platter. Melt another 2 tablespoons of Earth Balance in the skillet and continue dipping and cooking the remaining slices of bread. Transfer the remaining slices to the large platter when cooked.

3. Add the remaining tablespoon of Earth Balance to the skillet and swirl the skillet to coat the pan. Add the sliced bananas, blueberries, and maple syrup. Stir to coat and cook, stirring constantly, until bubbling and heated through, about 2–3 minutes. Spoon the maple bananas and blueberries evenly over the French Toast and serve immediately.

Avocado Confetti Tartine

As we all know, avocado toast had a meteor-like rise in the food world. Somehow, I didn't get it. Toast with avocado spread on top? So we decided to up the game a bit by creating this heartier, more colorful, and even healthier version, which is wildly popular on our menu—and it's so beautiful to serve! We make our tartine on a delicious grilled baguette and use our guacamole in place of the sliced plain avocado; it has minced red onions in it and a little olive oil for even more flavor and nutrition. Then we top it with a selection of colorful, halved organic heirloom grape tomatoes and drizzle it with our Lemon-Garlic Dressing (page 35) for even more flavor, pizzazz, and nutrients. I hope you'll enjoy this for breakfast or lunch, or even for a light dinner on a hot summer evening, perhaps with a bountiful salad with chickpeas and walnuts on top for a delicious protein to balance your meal. Or top your tartine with an olive oil–fried organic egg or two. Multiply the recipe to make as many servings as you please.

Serves 2

olive oil spray

1 9-inch baguette, cut in half lengthwise

1 cup guacamole

16 colorful organic heirloom grape tomatoes, cut in half lengthwise

sea salt and pepper

1 tablespoon Lemon-Garlic Dressing

Heat a grill pan over medium heat. Spray the cut side of the baguette halves with olive oil spray. Spray the pan with olive oil spray. Place the baguette halves, cut side down, onto the heated and sprayed pan. Using a large metal spatula, gently press the baguette to slightly flatten the halves, and cook for about 2–3 minutes, until the undersides are golden when lifted with the metal spatula. Transfer the baguette halves to a platter. Using a rubber spatula or a butter knife, spread half of the guacamole over each half of the baguette. Arrange the grape tomato halves evenly over the guacamole. Sprinkle lightly with sea salt and pepper. Drizzle the dressing evenly over the top of each half and serve.

Lemon-Garlic Dressing and Drizzle

This simple, fresh and lemony, vitamin C–filled dressing is a perfect example of why freshness matters! The flavors of lemon and garlic, with good olive oil, come through whether you are drizzling it over our Avocado Confetti Tartine or onto a simple salad of organic romaine, tomatoes, red onions, red peppers, carrots, and chickpeas—my go-to salad combination. And it really brightens any roasted vegetable dish as well. Drizzle away!

Makes about 1 cup

½ cup extra-virgin olive oil

½ cup freshly squeezed lemon juice, from about 3 lemons

5 cloves garlic, sliced

salt and pepper to taste

1. Measure the ingredients into a blender cup. Cover and blend on high speed for about 15–20 seconds, until smooth. Taste for seasoning.

2. Store in a covered, labeled, and dated jar for up to a week.

Vegan Breakfast Sandwich

Breakfast sandwiches are ubiquitous! We came up with this delicious combination of toasted slices of multigrain bread, sautéed GMO-free vegan sausage (we use Tofurky brand in our kitchen), sautéed organic arugula (spinach or Tuscan kale would work as well), slices of avocado, and our Chili Vinaigrette. It's a wonderful and totally satisfying breakfast, lunch, or dinner sandwich. Just add some roasted organic potatoes or your favorite sides for a satisfying lunch or dinner. Multiply the recipe to make as many sandwiches as you need.

Makes 1 sandwich

2 slices multigrain bread

olive oil spray

1 tablespoon extra-virgin olive oil, divided

1 link vegan sausage, cut in half lengthwise, and again in half widthwise

1 cup organic arugula, Tuscan kale, or spinach

salt and pepper

½ avocado, sliced

2 teaspoons Chili Vinaigrette

1. Toast the sliced bread. Place the slices onto a plate, single layer. Heat a small skillet over medium heat. Spray the heated skillet with olive oil spray, then add ½ tablespoon olive oil. Add the sausage, cut side down, and heat for about 1 minute on each side—it's already cooked, so it just needs to heat through. You can test this by inserting a metal fork into the center, then carefully touching the tines—if they are hot, the sausage is hot. Transfer the sausage halves to one slice of toast.

2. Heat the remaining olive oil in the small skillet. Add the arugula or other greens you are using. Sprinkle lightly with salt and pepper (the sausages tend to be salty) and cook, using tongs to toss for about 2 minutes, until wilted. Transfer the cooked greens over the sausage. Arrange the sliced avocado over the cooked greens. Drizzle with the Chili Vinaigrette. Top with the second slice of toast and enjoy.

Chili Vinaigrette

This is the dressing we drizzle onto our Vegan Breakfast Sandwich and our black bean, corn, and bell pepper Puebla Salad, but this smokey, orange-flavored dressing is delicious on any tossed salad or drizzled on grilled vegetables, too.

Makes about 1½ cups

1 cup orange juice, freshly squeezed is best, but store-bought will do fine

½ cup GMO-free organic canola oil

4 cloves garlic, sliced

1 tablespoon smoked paprika

salt and pepper to taste

Combine the ingredients into a blender cup. Cover and blend on high speed for about 30 seconds, until smooth. Taste for seasonings. Store in a labeled and dated glass jar. Cover and store in the refrigerator for up to a week.

Fruit and Nut Granola

Claire's Corner Copia

Handmade in our kitchen, using organic and gluten-free oats, apple juice, and other sustainable ingredients. Bring some home for breakfast or to work or on your hike for a quality snack.

Granola

Granola has become more prevalent, and we love that because it's a terrific breakfast cereal and a great snack for hiking and after school. It's also a perfect gift to bring a coworker, classmate, or teacher. I can't remember a time at Claire's Corner Copia when we didn't make granola! Right now, we're using gluten-free oats because everyone can eat these oats and we really like that.

Make a batch or two, and once it's cooled to room temperature it'll be good for a couple of weeks stored at room temperature. We sell 2-cup portions and they fly off the shelf. It's that good.

Serves 8

6 cups rolled gluten-free oats

¼ cup sunflower seeds

¼ cup sliced almonds

¼ cup pumpkin seeds

¼ cup walnut halves

¼ cup unsweetened coconut

2 teaspoons cinnamon

2 teaspoons ground ginger

½ cup apple cider

¼ cup GMO-free canola oil

½ cup agave

olive oil spray

½ cup dried cranberries

1. Preheat the oven to 250 degrees. Using two spoons, toss the oats, sunflower seeds, almonds, pumpkin seeds, walnuts, and coconut. Sprinkle the cinnamon and ginger evenly over the top and toss to mix.

2. In a separate bowl, whisk together the cider, oil, and agave. Pour this evenly over the oat mixture, using a rubber spatula to scrape the bowl. Using two spoons, toss well to coat evenly.

3. Spray two rectangular baking dishes with olive oil spray. Turn the granola onto the baking dishes, using a rubber spatula to scrape the bowl and to spread evenly. Bake uncovered for about 2 hours, stirring occasionally, until the mixture feels dry to the touch. After an hour, rotate the baking dishes to bake evenly. Add the dried cranberries and stir carefully to combine. Cool to room temperature, then store in tightly covered containers at room temperature. I love to use glass Ball jars for mine.

Tofu Scramble

Tofu scrambles are a terrific and delicious way to enjoy an easy vegan, protein-filled breakfast, lunch, or dinner. It's a one-pan meal that offers so much variety depending on what seasonal vegetables you use. The most popular combination at Claire's includes organic kale, tomatoes, black olives, and red onion. Get creative and enjoy the rainbow by mixing it up with broccoli, spinach, asparagus, and other delicious vegetables. Tofu scrambles are great with a side of good bread or roasted organic potatoes and fresh seasonal fruit.

Serves 4

1 14-ounce package organic firm tofu, drained

olive oil spray

5 tablespoons extra-virgin olive oil

1 small red onion, cut in half and then into thin slices

salt and pepper

2 teaspoons dried oregano

1 small bunch organic Tuscan kale, tough stems removed and discarded and leaves and tender stems finely chopped

2 large organic tomatoes, cut in half and coarsely chopped, include juices

½ cup sliced black olives

3 tablespoons Lemon-Garlic Dressing

1. Turn the drained tofu into a bowl, and, using a potato masher, mash the tofu into tiny pieces. Drain again.

2. Spray a large skillet with olive oil spray, then place it over medium heat. Add the olive oil and swirl the skillet to coat the bottom of the pan. Add the red onion and sprinkle with salt and pepper and the oregano. Stir to coat and cook for a minute to flavor the oil.

3. Add the chopped kale, tomatoes, drained tofu, and olives. Cook for about 7–10 minutes, stirring frequently, until the kale is tender and the tofu heated through.

4. Drizzle with the dressing and taste for seasoning. Serve hot.

smoothies and sweet drinks

We've been making giant smoothies at Claire's Corner Copia for as long as I can remember. I recall first hearing about them from a customer who went to a World's Fair and drank them there. We love them! They are a terrific way to get your fruits and vegetables each day. And we especially love how the kiddos who come to Claire's enjoy them. Over the years, we've expanded fresh fruit smoothies to include more dynamic ingredients. We've built upon some of our original ingredients while also eliminating others to allow for more health-conscious options. For example, we removed wheat germ because gluten-free allergies became more prevalent. Our decisions are always backed by research, and as research provided more data on certain foods, we updated the ingredients in our menu with you in mind. A big example of this is adding organic kale to our smoothie menu when kale went from a garnish in the deli to the queen of super greens. (Talk about a successful marketing campaign—kudos to the kale folks.) Another deliciously proven trick we've incorporated is buying frozen fruits and defrost-ing them. Frozen fruits are more consistently sweet and available. Try it, it really works! Fresh organic strawberries actually get sweeter when frozen and defrosted. Further, we've always believed in giving you choices between dairy and vegan, and while we've lessened the dairy choices and increased the vegan ones, it will always be your choice. As we believe, it's the experience of the journey and not just the destination, and our customers like to sip their way to healthy ingredients when they are on the move, and that's why we make 24-ounce smoothies!

So however you move and whatever you choose, let our smoothie ingredients fuel your journey.

And remember to have a little fun along the way. As we always say, "There is room for indulgences in a healthy diet, but there is no room for a healthy diet in one filled with indulgences!" In other words, a little something sweet is an acceptable treat after a healthy meal.

Enjoy!

Homemade Ginger Ale Syrup

Once you've had homemade ginger ale, you won't settle for one that has been premade months ago! We always use organic ginger because it's better for you and for the environment. Ginger is spicy and delicious. It is good for the gastrointestinal system, and it's often used to relieve nausea, something anyone who has been pregnant appreciates. And when you really want a soda, homemade ginger ale is a delicious one to choose. This syrup will keep fresh in the refrigerator for up to two weeks. Make a batch of this syrup and do what we do: add it to San Pellegrino sparkling water! For each glass of ginger ale, put four to five ice cubes in a tall glass. Add a 8.45-ounce bottle of San Pellegrino sparkling mineral water and 3 tablespoons ginger ale syrup. Stir to combine. Enjoy this refreshing drink! But don't drink it too often—remember, it's high in sugar content and calories, so once in a while is an indulgence. Please save it for exactly that.

Makes about 1 cup, enough for 5 servings

1 cup water

1 1-inch piece fresh ginger, unpeeled, sliced thin

1 cup packed brown sugar

1. Combine the water and the sliced ginger in a blender cup. Cover and blend on high speed for about 1 minute, until well blended.

2. Pour the mixture into a small heavy pot, using a rubber spatula to scrape the blender cup and lid. Add the brown sugar and whisk to combine. Place over medium-high heat. Cook for a couple of minutes, whisking frequently, until it comes to a boil. Reduce the heat to low and simmer for 2 minutes, whisking frequently.

3. Turn off the heat and let the syrup cool to room temperature before storing it in a glass jar. Be sure to label and date it.

Kale a Bunga Smoothie

One morning at Claire's, we were "playing" with ideas for a new smoothie and this is what we came up with. When it came time to choose a name, our manager Margie said, "Kale a Bunga, man," and we all laughed—and loved it. This drink is delicious and it has the super foods, kale and blueberries, with potassium from the banana, too. It's very popular and we're proud to sell it.

Makes one 12-ounce smoothie

1 cup ice cubes

1 cup pineapple juice

1 cup coarsely chopped organic Tuscan kale, packed

⅓ cup organic blueberries, fresh or defrosted frozen berries

1 ripe banana

Combine the ingredients into a blender cup in the order listed. Cover and blend on high speed for about 1 minute or until fully blended. Pour into a tall glass and sip away.

Claire's
CORNER COPIA

A Vegetarian Restaurant since 1975
1000 Chapel Street – New Haven, CT. 06510
Telephone 203-562-3888
Web Address www.clairescornercopia.com
Sustainable, Global, Vegetarian, Since 1975

The Greener the Cleaner Smoothie

This delicious smoothie is so hydrating and refreshing. Some people add a ¼ cup scoop of our organic and vegan hemp protein. Either way, it's a great snack, or breakfast or lunch smoothie.

Makes one 24-ounce smoothie

1 cup ice cubes

1 cup pineapple juice

½ avocado

6 ½-inch thick organic cucumber slices

1 large stalk organic celery with leaves, separated into three

1 cup organic baby spinach, packed

¼ cup pineapple chunks, frozen or fresh

¼ cup organic parsley, leaves and stems, coarsely chopped

Measure the ingredients into a blender cup in the order listed. Cover and blend for about 1 minute, or until blended and smooth. Pour into a large glass and relax!

Claire's
CORNER COPIA
A Vegetarian Restaurant since 1975
1000 Chapel Street – New Haven, CT. 06510
Telephone 203-562-3888
Web Address www.clairescornercopia.com
Sustainable, Global, Vegetarian, Since 1975

Carrot Top Smoothie

This is our offering to our regulars who come in and ask for carrot juice. Blending allows us to enjoy all the health benefits without extracting the fiber when juicing. And this drink is gorgeous! Bright orange and so delicious. Super healthy, too, with beta carotene, fiber, and vitamins A and C. Your precious eyes will be "looking out" for carrots.

Makes one 24-ounce smoothie

1 cup ice cubes

1 cup freshly squeezed orange juice—we use Natalie's Orchard (a small family-owned farm in Florida)

½ cup ripe mango, fresh or defrosted frozen mango chunks

1 large carrot, sliced into ¼-inch slices

Measure the ingredients into a blender cup in the order listed. Cover and blend for a minute or two, until smooth and creamy. Enjoy every drop!

Vita Mita Smoothie

Many years ago, a man named Keo used to come in with his guitar. He came to Yale to teach a seminar about once a month, and each time he'd come to Claire's Corner Copia and play a song using all the customer names we called out. At Claire's, we take your order and your name, and when your meal is ready, we call out your name; you raise your hand and we bring you your meal. It's much more fun, I think, to have a song sung each time, but there will likely never be another Keo. Then again, our place really is pretty magical!

This smoothie has so few ingredients, but it's very delicious, smooth, and creamy.

Makes one 24-ounce smoothie

1 cup ice cubes

½ ripe avocado

1 ripe banana, broken into three

1 cup organic soy milk

1 tablespoon honey

Measure the ingredients into a blender cup in the order listed. Blend on high speed for about 1 minute, or until smooth and creamy. Enjoy it!

Mango Lassi

Anjul Dutt worked at Claire's Corner Copia back in the day, and we've remained friends (even across the pond) over the years. She lives in England but she's from India, where lassi drinks originated. We use our homemade organic plain yogurt for this drink, but at home, I use store-bought in a pinch. Either way, it's refreshing and delicious, protein and calcium rich. We use organic 2 percent milk to make our yogurt, but either skim or whole is fine for this drink. You choose!

Makes one 16-ounce lassi

1 cup ice cubes

1 cup plain organic yogurt

½ cup mango chunks, fresh or defrosted frozen

½ teaspoon ground cardamom

1 tablespoon honey (optional)

Measure the ingredients into a blender cup in the order listed. Cover and blend on high speed for about 1 minute, or until well blended and smooth. Enjoy!

Yogurt

We make our own organic yogurt pretty much every day at Claire's Corner Copia! It's creamy and we know exactly what goes into it: organic milk and a little organic yogurt to "proof" it. That's it. And if you make your own yogurt, say once every week or so, you'll save a lot of money, too. That savings can be used to buy the best, organic fruits and vegetables—because we all know how much they cost. We also know that we're worth it. My mother always said, "Never cheat your stomach!" I like to top my yogurt with organic berries, maybe some ground flax seeds, and chopped Brazil nuts, walnuts, or almonds, and when I desire a little sweetness, I drizzle a little maple syrup over the top.

I like to make the yogurt before bed because it's ready for breakfast the next day.

Makes about 16 cups

1 gallon organic 2 percent milk
   (that's what we use in our kitchen)

⅔ cup plain whole or low-fat organic
   yogurt

1. Heat the milk in a large, uncovered pot over medium heat without stirring until it begins to foam up. When the foam reaches about halfway to the top of the pot, in about 15 minutes, remove the pan from the heat.

2. Pour the heated milk into a large glass bowl. Set the bowl on the counter to cool to the point where you can insert your pinkie finger into the center of the bowl comfortably for 10 seconds—we never use a thermometer; your finger works fine.

3. Measure the ⅔ cup of yogurt into a medium-size bowl. Add ⅓ cup of the heated milk into the bowl with the yogurt and stir well to combine.

4. Pour the yogurt mixture into the heated milk and stir lightly with a rubber spatula. Use a plate to cover the bowl without touching the yogurt. Now, wrap the bowl with a thick towel—you want to allow the milk to cool slowly. Leave the wrapped bowl on the counter by the stove, undisturbed for 8 hours.

5. After the 8 hours, remove the towel. Remove ⅔ cup of yogurt, label and date it, and set it aside for your next batch. Spoon the remaining yogurt into glass jars, cover, and date. Enjoy your yogurt!

Chocolate Syrup

Measure a cup of your favorite milk into a glass and stir in 4 tablespoons of this chocolate syrup for a delicious chocolate milk. Or, for hot chocolate, heat a cup of milk and stir in the chocolate syrup.

Makes 2 cups syrup

2 cups water

1 cup unsweetened cocoa powder, we use Hershey's

½ cup packed brown sugar

½ cup granulated sugar

1. Measure the ingredients into a small, heavy pot and whisk to combine. Place over high heat and bring to a boil, whisking continuously. Once it comes to a boil, reduce the heat to low and continue whisking for another minute.

2. Remove from the heat and cool to room temperature before storing in a labeled glass jar for up to two weeks. That is, unless you are making hot chocolate right away.

Girl's Sick Tea

Many years ago, a few girls, undergrads from Yale University, came in when they weren't feeling well and asked if we could make them something for their colds. We made this drink, and just like that, it became a thing! Other girls came in for this drink, for themselves or for their friends who were sick in the dorms, and we dubbed it the Girl's Sick Tea. Before long, boys started coming in, whispering, "Can I get the Girl's Sick Tea?" This was all before we even made a sign to advertise it. Today, it's become a year-round drink, served hot or iced, and it's popular among those not feeling well and those feeling just fine. It's lemony and gingery, and if you love turmeric, it's your drink! It's loaded with antioxidants, too.

Makes one 16-ounce cup

1 inch fresh organic ginger, sliced into thin slices

½ inch fresh organic turmeric, sliced into thin slices

½ organic lemon, cut into thin slices, seeds discarded

a sprinkle of cayenne

2 tablespoons honey

1 cup boiling water, plus 1 cup hot or cold water

ice cubes (optional)

1. Place the ginger, turmeric, lemon slices, cayenne, and honey into a blender cup in the order listed. Add the boiling water. Cover and blend on high speed for about 2 minutes, until fully blended.

2. Pour into a large cup, add remaining hot or cold water, and stir well to combine. If serving cold, pour into a large glass with ice cubes.

Hibiscus Syrup

I first discovered dried hibiscus flowers many years ago at a food show in New York City. I was smitten! The color is a vibrant, crimson red, and I love the tart, cranberry-raspberry flavor. I ordered organic hibiscus flowers before I even left the display booth! We use dried organic hibiscus flowers to color our frostings, as a tea, and for this syrup that we use for our flavored lemonades and Italian sodas. Just pour some into your favorite drink or a glass of Pellegrino water for a tart and sweet splurge. It's delicious poured into a glass of prosecco, too. Make a batch and store it in the fridge for up to two weeks. Remember to label and date it.

Makes about 3¼ cups

2½ cups water

2 cups sugar

½ cup dried organic hibiscus flowers

1. Measure the water and sugar into a small heavy pot. Whisk well to combine. Bring to a boil over high heat, then reduce the heat to medium and occasionally whisk at a simmer for about 2 minutes, until the sugar is dissolved into the water.

2. Stir in the hibiscus flowers and cover the pot. Turn off the heat and let sit for about an hour, stirring occasionally. Uncover the pot and keep the pot on the stove to continue cooling down.

3. Place a mesh strainer into a bowl in the sink. Ladle the hot Hibiscus Syrup into the strainer, using the back of the ladle to press out as much liquid as possible. Discard the flowers.

4. Let the syrup cool to room temperature before storing in the fridge for up to a week. I like to use glass jars. Be sure to label and date it! Have fun!

Lemonade

My mother always had fresh lemons in the refrigerator. And after I visited her father's birthplace, I understood why she so loved lemons. Lemons grew in great abundance in Amalfi, Italy, where my maternal grandparents were born, so lemons were always used in recipes from drinks to desserts, pastas, entrees, and vegetable dishes when my mother was a child, and she continued the tradition with our family. Today, I do the same! Lemonade is a perfect summer drink, citrusy enough to quench your thirst and just sweet enough to make you want to drink it all summer long. I like my lemonade on the tart side, but if you prefer a sweeter lemonade, add 3 tablespoons of sugar rather than 2. This recipe is for one glass, but you can do what we do and prepare it by the gallon for a crowd.

Makes one 12-ounce glass

¼ cup water, plus 1 cup water

2 tablespoons granulated sugar

3 tablespoons freshly squeezed lemon juice, from about 1 lemon

3–4 ice cubes

1. Measure ¼ cup water and 2 tablespoons sugar into a small pot. Place over high heat for about 30–40 seconds, stirring constantly, until the sugar is dissolved into the water. Remove from the heat. Stir in the remaining water and the lemon juice.

2. Place the ice cubes into a tall glass. Pour the contents of the pot over the ice cubes and stir to combine. Enjoy it!

Frozen Lemonade BMG

Maria Garcia Huidobro came here from Chile with her husband, who was at the Yale Drama School. She is a physical therapist in Chile, but for the two years she was here in the States, she was the nicest barista here at Claire's Corner Copia. One hot summer day, she suggested we make this drink she enjoyed in Chile. That's how the BMG was added to our menu, and it remains a most popular drink. It's a delicious frozen drink and it's so refreshing, made with our lemonade plus basil, mint, and organic ginger. By the end of March, sometimes even before, we're clamoring for this drink, but our manager Rosie keeps us in check and we wait until April to add it back to our drinks menu. It's worth the wait! This recipe is for one 16-ounce glass, but you can double or triple it for a larger batch. Be sure to drink it within an hour, or it just isn't the same.

Makes one tall glass, about 16 ounces

1 cup ice cubes

1½ cups fresh lemonade

¼ cup fresh, organic basil leaves and tender stems

5–6 sprigs of fresh, organic mint leaves and tender stems (spearmint or peppermint)

½ inch fresh organic ginger, sliced into thin slices

Measure the ingredients into a blender cup, in the order listed. Cover and blend on high speed for about 1–2 minutes, or until the ice is blended into a slushy-looking drink. Enjoy!

Neapolitan Smoothie

After a crazy busy weekend, we sometimes celebrate with an ice cream party on Monday. I order everyone's favorite flavor and we each take home a pint. Cele, our long-time favorite kitchen king, loves Neapolitan ice cream. The problem for us is that it's become nearly impossible to find that combination these days, so we came up with this drink for Cele! We hope you'll enjoy it as much as we do.

Makes one 24-ounce smoothie

1 cup ice cubes

1 cup chocolate oat milk

1 large, ripe banana, broken into three pieces

½ cup strawberries, defrosted frozen, including their juices

¼ cup chocolate syrup

Measure the ingredients into a blender cup in the order listed. Cover and blend on high speed for about 1 minute, or until well blended and creamy. Pour into a big glass. Enjoy the coolness!

Dickie's Bulldog Smoothie

Dickie was a freshman at Yale University and he was on the football team. His mom came in with him one day and asked if we could create a smoothie that was loaded with protein but low in cholesterol—"I'm afraid Dickie will eat steaks and burgers every day for protein!" We went to work and created this smoothie in his name. For years, Dickie brought in friends and dates to show his namesake smoothie. Reason number gazillion why I love this place! It's the people!

Makes one 24-ounce smoothie

1 cup ice cubes

1 cup organic soymilk

1 cup organic plain yogurt

¼ cup organic protein powder, or less, depending on the serving size

1 large ripe banana, broken into three pieces

honey or agave for sweetness (optional)

Place the ingredients into a blender cup, in the order listed. Cover and blend on high speed for a minute, or until blended and creamy. Pour into a tall glass and sip away.

Claire's
CORNER COPIA

A Vegetarian Restaurant since 1975
1000 Chapel Street – New Haven, CT. 06510
Telephone 203-562-3888
Web Address www.clairescornercopia.com
Sustainable, Global, Vegetarian, Since 1975

Strawberries and Cream Smoothie

This is the prettiest drink! Pink and creamy, and delicious either with dairy milk and whipped cream or vegan milk and vegan whipped cream. Enjoy it on a hot summer day!

Makes one 24-ounce smoothie

1 cup ice cubes

1 cup half-and-half, or vegan cream (we use Violife brand)

1 tablespoon pure vanilla powder (we avoid alcohol in respect to our customers who avoid it)

1 heaping cup defrosted frozen organic strawberries (they are sweeter unless you have organic sweet summer strawberries)

whipped cream, dairy or vegan (again, we use Violife)

Measure the ice cubes, half-and-half, vanilla, and strawberries into a blender cup in the order listed. Cover and blend on high speed for about 1 minute, until blended and creamy. Pour into a tall glass and top with whipped cream. Sip away!

soups, salads, dressings, dips, and drizzles

Soups and salads have always been the foundation of our menu. Everyone loves our soups, and our customers also love our salads because, like our soups, they are bountiful and delicious, and they offer tremendous opportunities to get you to the recommended seven to nine servings of fruits and vegetables every day. Personally, I don't feel like I've eaten well unless I've had a good salad—every single day! Mix it up—add your favorite greens and vegetables, maybe some nuts and dried cherries or cranberries, with a handful of beans or whole grains (like cooked chickpeas or lentils, black beans, or quinoa). Have fun, mix it up, and eat your way to better health.

Potato and Corn Chowder

This delicious soup is extremely popular at Claire's, but because it's so rich, we make it less frequently than our bean and vegetable soups. It's creamy and so delicious—irresistible! Vegan or dairy, we have fans on both sides. You choose.

Serves 4

⅓ cup vegan or dairy butter, cut into pieces

1 large yellow onion, coarsely chopped

6 cloves garlic, sliced thin

¼ cup Italian flat-leaf parsley, finely chopped

6 large organic Yukon Gold potatoes, peeled and cut into a medium dice

salt and pepper

4 cups water

½ teaspoon dried thyme

½ teaspoon nutmeg

2 cups frozen corn

1 quart Violife vegan heavy cream (any vegan heavy cream is fine) or dairy heavy cream

2 cups vegan or dairy milk

1. Melt the butter over low heat in a large pot. Add the onion, garlic, parsley, and potatoes. Sprinkle with salt and pepper. Cover and cook for about 30 minutes, stirring frequently. Lower the heat if the potatoes start to stick.

2. Add the water, thyme, nutmeg, and corn. Raise the heat to medium. Cover and bring to a low boil. Cook at a low boil for about 30 minutes, stirring frequently, until the potatoes are fork-tender.

3. Stir in the milk and heavy cream. Cook, uncovered, at a low boil, stirring frequently for about 15 minutes until heated through. Taste for seasonings.

Turkish Red Lentil Soup

This soup is always a big hit at the restaurant and at home. Why not? It's loaded with the flavor of red lentils, which actually turn yellow after cooking—who knew! It also has blended carrots, onions, garlic, potatoes, arborio rice, spices, and a lemony hit at the end. Serve it with warm Greek pita or whole wheat pita for dipping.

Serves 6

4 quarts water

1 pound red lentils, sorted for stones, then rinsed in a colander and drained

½ cup extra-virgin olive oil

5 medium carrots, coarsely chopped

2 medium yellow onions, coarsely chopped

4 medium organic Yukon Gold potatoes, peeled and coarsely chopped

1 small bunch Italian flat-leaf parsley, coarsely chopped

6 cloves garlic, coarsely chopped

3 tablespoons tomato paste (you can label and freeze the remaining in a small BPA-free ziplock bag)

1 tablespoon za'atar seasoning

1 tablespoon ground cumin

salt and pepper

½ cup arborio rice

1 lemon, freshly squeezed, about 3 tablespoons

1. Measure water into a heavy 8-quart pot. Add the lentils and the olive oil. Cover and bring to a boil over high heat.

2. Meanwhile, turn the carrots, onions, potatoes, parsley, and garlic into the bowl of a food processor fitted with a metal blade and process for about 20 seconds, or until the vegetables are in tiny pieces.

3. Add the vegetable mixture to the pot with the lentils. Then add the tomato paste, za'atar, cumin, a little salt and pepper, and the rice. Stir to combine.

4. Cover the pot and bring to a boil, then reduce the heat to low and cook at a low boil, stirring frequently for about 25 minutes, until the rice and vegetables are soft and melted into the soup.

5. Taste for salt and add as needed. Stir in the lemon juice. Taste for seasonings.

Red Bean, Tomato, and Spinach Soup—AKA Rosie's Fave

This super healthy soup is our manager Rosie's favorite, and it's loaded with protein, fiber, vitamin C, and iron. It's delicious any time of year, especially during those cold, winter months when you really want a hot bowl of a rich soup. Serve it with good Italian bread (garlic bread would be yummy) and a salad made with seasonal vegetables.

Note: We never really know how old dry beans are because we don't know how long they've been sitting on the shelf at the grocery store, so cooking times can vary.

Serves 6

1 pound red kidney beans, sorted for stones, and rinsed

2 medium red onions, cut in half then sliced into medium ribs

6 cloves garlic, sliced thin

1 small bunch Italian flat-leaf parsley

2 bay leaves

½ cup extra-virgin olive oil

2 teaspoons fennel seeds

10 large fresh basil leaves

1 tablespoon dried cumin

2 teaspoons dried oregano

1 teaspoon crushed red pepper flakes

1 35-ounce can whole peeled San Marzano tomatoes, squeezed with your hands to crush

1 6-ounce can tomato paste

salt and pepper to taste

1 11-ounce container organic spinach

1. Bring 4 quarts of water to boil in a heavy 8-quart pot over high heat. Add the sorted kidney beans, onions, garlic, parsley, bay leaves, olive oil, fennel seeds, fresh basil leaves, cumin, oregano, and crushed red pepper flakes. Cover, raise the heat to high, and bring to a boil.

2. Reduce the heat to medium and cook, covered, at a low-medium boil for about 1 to 1½ hours, depending on how dry/hard the beans are, stirring occasionally, until the beans are barely tender.

3. Add the tomatoes, tomato paste, and salt and pepper. Cover, raise the heat to high, and again bring to a boil. Then reduce the heat to medium-low and continue cooking, covered, at a low boil, stirring occasionally for about 1 hour, until the beans are tender.

4. Stir in the spinach, cover, and continue cooking at a low-medium boil for about 30 minutes, until the spinach is soft and has flavored the broth. Taste for seasonings.

Chilled Gazpacho

This chunky soup had been our summer staple for decades! We occasionally make other chilled soups, but none are as popular as this one—and why not? Summer tomatoes are here only for summer. Serve this soup the day you prepare it for the best, freshest flavors. We like to serve it with corn tortillas or corn tortilla chips. Happy summer!

Serves 4

4 large, ripe tomatoes, any variety will be wonderful, cut into thin wedges

2 medium cucumbers, coarsely chopped

2 medium red bell peppers, seeded and coarsely chopped

½ small red onion, coarsely chopped

2 cloves garlic, coarsely chopped

1 small bunch Italian flat-leaf parsley, coarsely chopped

¼ cup extra-virgin olive oil

1 tablespoon red wine vinegar

juice from 1 lemon, about 3 tablespoons

salt and pepper

¼ cup bread crumbs

1. Place the tomatoes, cucumbers, bell peppers, onion, garlic, parsley, olive oil, vinegar, and lemon juice into a big bowl. Season with salt and pepper. Stir to combine.

2. Ladle the mixture into a food processor fitted with a metal blade. Cover and process for about 15–20 seconds (depending on your processor), until chunky but finely chopped. Turn the mixture into a large bowl as you process the ingredients.

3. Taste for seasonings. Stir in the bread crumbs. Serve immediately or chill for up to 8 hours.

Irish Cabbage Soup

Everyone at Claire's has their favorite menu items. This soup is our manager Ashley's favorite! It's a clear broth soup, with loads of healthy cabbage, cauliflower, and potatoes. It's more like a soup-stew, so it's filling and satisfying. And it's a must on Saint Patrick's Day! This and our Irish soda bread.

Serves 6

½ cup extra-virgin olive oil

2 tablespoons vegan butter (we use Earth Balance organic)

2 large yellow onions, cut in half then into medium slices

4 large organic russett potatoes, peeled and cut into ¾-inch cubes

2 large heads Savoy cabbage, cored and coarsely chopped

1 large head cauliflower, florets separated and coarsely chopped

1 small bunch parsley, coarsely chopped

2 bay leaves

2 tablespoons caraway seeds

salt and pepper

2 quarts water

1. Measure the olive oil and vegan butter into an 8-quart heavy pot. Add the remaining ingredients except the water. Place over low-medium heat and cover. Cook the vegetables, stirring frequently, for about 30 minutes, until the vegetables are softened but not at all brown.

2. Add the water and stir to combine. Cover and bring to a boil over high heat, then reduce the heat to medium; keep covered and cook at a medium boil, stirring frequently, for about 45 minutes, until the vegetables are soft and the broth is rich. Taste for seasonings.

Cream of Tomato Soup

This soup is a perennial favorite, especially on those rainy days when WTNH chief meteorologist Gil Simmons suggests tomato soup with a Grilled Cheese Sandwich (page 99). Make this delicious soup dairy or vegan, depending on the crowd. We alternate at Claire's because we have fans on both sides. Sometimes we serve this soup a little chunky, and other times we blend the soup before adding the cream—again, we have fans on both sides. Please be careful if you blend the hot soup. Hot liquids expand, and the hot liquid can "jump" up and burn you—and make a mess—so blend a half blender at a time, cover the top of the blender with a dish towel, wear oven mitts, and keep your face away from the blender. I speak from experience!

Makes about 3 quarts

2 large yellow onions, coarsely chopped

2 shallots, coarsely chopped

1 large carrot, coarsely chopped

1 small bunch Italian flat-leaf parsley, coarsely chopped

6 cloves garlic, sliced

5 large basil leaves

½ cup butter, dairy or vegan, cut into slices

salt and pepper

a few shakes of cayenne

2 28-ounce cans whole peeled San Marzano tomatoes in juice, squeezed with your hands to crush

1 small can, about 6 ounces, of tomato paste

2 cups water

2 cups dairy or vegan heavy cream (we use Violife brand)

¼ cup finely chopped fresh dill

1. Place the chopped onions, shallots, carrots, parsley, garlic, and basil leaves in the bowl of a food processor fitted with a metal blade. Cover and process for 30 seconds, until the mixture is finely minced.

2. Place the butter and the processed vegetables into a heavy 8-quart pot over medium heat; sprinkle with salt and pepper and a few shakes of cayenne. Cover and cook, stirring frequently, for about 35 minutes, until the vegetables are soft. Add the tomatoes and their juices, the tomato paste, and the water. Stir well to combine. Raise the heat to medium-high. Cover the pot and bring to a boil, then lower the heat, stirring frequently at a simmer for about 35 minutes, until the tomatoes taste cooked.

3. Slowly stir in the cream, stirring constantly. Stir in the chopped dill. Taste for seasonings.

Creamy Vegan Potato Salad

This is the delicious salad we serve with our vegan Buffalo Tofu Wings (page 103), BBQ anything, and sometimes as a side for our sandwiches. It's a perennial favorite! We always start with organic Yukon Gold or red-skinned potatoes.

Serves 4–6

salt

6 large organic potatoes, peeled and cut into ¾-inch cubes

2 tablespoons white vinegar

1 medium organic red or orange bell pepper, seeded and finely chopped

2 large ribs organic celery, cut into thin slices

½ small red onion, peeled and finely chopped

¾ cup vegan mayonnaise

1 small bunch dill, rinsed and finely chopped, including any tender stems

salt and pepper

1. Bring a covered pot of lightly salted water to a boil over high heat. Carefully add the potatoes. Cover and return to a boil; then, remove the lid and boil for about 10 minutes until fork-tender.

2. Drain and turn the potatoes into a large bowl. Sprinkle the white vinegar evenly over the cooked potatoes, and, using two big spoons, gently toss to coat.

3. Add the remaining ingredients, including a little salt and pepper, and toss gently to combine. Taste for seasonings. Serve at room temperature or chilled.

Kale Crunch Salad

This super food salad is ever popular at Claire's! We love that it's so healthy and delicious and that our customers love it. It has organic Tuscan kale, brussels sprouts, chickpeas, pumpkin seeds, dried cranberries, and a mustardy cider vinaigrette. Even people who don't ordinarily like raw kale like this salad—truth be told, I'm one of those people!

Serves 4

1 medium bunch organic Tuscan kale, dry bottom ends removed and discarded, leaves and thinner stems cut into fairly thin slices

6 small-medium brussels sprouts, thinly sliced

2 cups chickpeas (we cook the dry chickpeas at Claire's, but you can use organic canned chickpeas, drained, like I do at home)

½ cup shelled pumpkin seeds

¼ cup dried cranberries

¼ cup extra-virgin olive oil

2 tablespoons cider vinegar

1 shallot, cut into quarters

2 teaspoons dried thyme

1 tablespoon Dijon mustard

2 tablespoons agave

salt and pepper

1. Cut off the dry 1 inch or so bottom ends of the kale stems and discard (or compost them like we do). Then cut the leaves and thinner stems into fairly thin slices and place in a large bowl. Add the sliced brussels sprouts, chickpeas, pumpkin seeds, and dried cranberries.

2. Measure the olive oil, cider vinegar, shallot quarters, thyme, mustard, and agave into the cup of a blender to make the dressing. Add a little salt and pepper. Cover and blend on high speed until well blended. Taste for seasonings.

3. Pour the contents of the blender over the bowl of kale and use a rubber spatula to scrape the contents of the blender—you don't want to waste any of this delicious dressing. Using two big spoons, toss the salad to combine the ingredients and coat with dressing. Taste for seasonings. Serve immediately or refrigerate for up to 8 hours—not much longer or it will wilt.

Sicilian Pistachio Pesto Pasta Salad

Pistachios have soared in popularity over the past few years. I'm not surprised. They are delicious and contain respectable amounts of protein, fiber, vitamin B6, iron, magnesium, and calcium—all good things. I love this pesto on a pasta salad or a potato salad, and it's also really good on the Kale Crunch Salad (page 81) in place of the mustardy cider vinaigrette. It makes a nice spread for crostini as well.

Serves 4

salt

1 pound of spaghetti, or your favorite pasta

¾ cup extra-virgin olive oil

3 cloves garlic, sliced

2 cups shelled pistachios, salted

zest of 1 lemon

1 teaspoon crushed red pepper flakes

black pepper

1. Cook the pasta in salted water according to package directions. Drain and rinse under cold water, then drain again. Turn into a large bowl.

2. Measure the olive oil into a blender cup. Add the garlic, pistachios, and lemon zest. Cover and blend on high speed until blended but a little chunky.

3. Pour this mixture onto the cooked pasta, using a rubber spatula to scrape the sides of the blender cup. Sprinkle the pepper flakes and a little black pepper evenly over the pasta. Don't add additional salt until you taste it later in the recipe because the pistachios are salted. Using two big spoons, toss to combine and coat the pasta with the pesto. Taste for seasonings. Serve at room temperature or chilled.

Quinoa Tabouli

Back in the day, we made our tabouli with bulgur wheat and people enjoyed it enough, but a couple of decades ago, we discovered quinoa. We loved that it tasted good, was loaded with protein, and was also gluten-free. We're always happy to find more ways to meet the needs of our beloved community, especially when it comes to allergies.

Serve this over organic arugula or romaine, or in a pita pocket sandwich with romaine, tomatoes, and tahini or other salad dressing.

Serves 4–6

1 pound quinoa, red or white

1 bunch Italian flat-leaf parsley, tough stems discarded, leaves and tender stems finely chopped

1 small red onion, finely chopped

¼ cup extra-virgin olive oil

⅓ cup lemon juice from about 1½ lemons (squeeze the other half into a glass of water for yourself)

1 tablespoon dried mint

salt and pepper

1. Measure the quinoa into a medium pot. Cover with water plus 2 inches; stir to mix. Cover the pot and bring to a boil over high heat; then reduce the heat to medium. Cook for about 10 minutes, stirring occasionally, until the quinoa is just tender and most of the water is absorbed. Turn into a large, shallow pan to cool to room temperature.

2. Once the quinoa is at room temperature, turn into a bowl. Add the parsley and onion, and, using two spoons, toss to combine.

3. Measure the olive oil, lemon juice, mint, and a little salt and pepper into a small bowl. Whisk to combine. Taste for seasonings.

4. Drizzle the dressing evenly over the quinoa mixture. Using two spoons, toss well to combine. Taste again for seasonings.

Truffled Parmesan Artichoke Hearts over Organic Arugula

This is one of those recipes that is so easy to prepare and so very delicious that I almost feel guilty when the compliments roll in.

Serves 4

1 14-ounce can artichoke hearts, quartered, drained

salt and pepper

2 tablespoons truffle oil

¼ cup grated Pecorino Romano cheese, plus additional if desired

1 5-ounce container organic arugula

16 organic grape tomatoes, cut in half lengthwise

3 tablespoons extra-virgin olive oil

3 tablespoons freshly squeezed organic lemon juice, from about 1 lemon

1. Turn the drained artichoke hearts into a small bowl. Sprinkle with salt and pepper. Drizzle with the truffle oil and the Pecorino Romano cheese. Using two spoons, toss to combine. Taste for seasonings.

2. Place the arugula into a medium bowl. Scatter the tomato halves evenly over the top. Drizzle evenly with the olive oil and the lemon juice, and sprinkle with salt and pepper. Using two spoons, toss to coat. Taste for seasonings.

3. Turn the arugula and tomatoes onto a platter. Spoon the truffled artichoke hearts evenly over the top. Sprinkle with additional Pecorino Romano cheese if desired. Serve immediately.

Minty Pumpkin Seed and Green Pea Pesto Pasta Salad

Pumpkin seeds and green peas add a healthy dose of protein, fiber, and magnesium to any dish—and that's all good news! We love when we can add these seeds to our salads and pestos. When dried, the peas along with the pumpkin seeds add a nice crunch to your oatmeal, too. I keep a jar of them right on my counter for snacking. They are super healthy. Your blood pressure, muscles, and nerve function will thank you. Sometimes we add broccoli florets to this dish—just to add to the flavor and nutrients. If you want to add broccoli, add the florets from one bunch during the last 2 minutes of cooking your pasta and drain it with the pasta.

Serves 4

1 pound rigatoni or spaghetti, or your favorite pasta

salt

1 10-ounce bag frozen green peas

1 4-ounce bunch organic mint, tough stems discarded, rinsed and drained

4 cloves garlic, sliced

1 cup shelled pumpkin seeds

salt and pepper

½ cup extra-virgin olive oil

juice from 1 lemon, about 3 tablespoons

1 jalapeño pepper, seeded and coarsely chopped (be sure to always wash your hands after handling hot peppers or you can burn your eyes and face if you touch them)

1. Cook your pasta in lightly salted boiling water according to package directions. Drain, then rinse under cold water and drain again. Turn into a large bowl.

2. Cook the peas according to package directions; drain, rinse under cold water, and drain again.

3. Place the cooked peas, mint, garlic, pumpkin seeds, a little salt and pepper, olive oil, lemon juice, and jalapeño pepper into the bowl of a food processor fitted with a metal blade. Cover and process for about 2–3 minutes, until the pesto is fairly smooth but still a bit chunky. Taste for seasonings.

4. Turn the pesto over the drained pasta, using a rubber spatula to scrape the processor bowl of all the delicious pesto. Using two spoons, toss the pasta and pesto to coat evenly. Taste for seasoning. Serve at room temperature or chilled.

Aji Amarillo Aioli

I was first introduced to aji amarillo decades ago when I hired a terrific student named Walker. He was from Peru, and his mother sent me aji amarillo as a thank you gift. Really, he was a gift to me! Walker now lives in Connecticut with his wife, and we love when he visits. Aji amarillo peppers have a lovely medium-hot heat with a fruity-floral taste, and I love them! They make your aioli a pretty golden color, too. If you can't find the dried chile pepper to soak, seed, and blend, buy the aji amarillo powder. This aioli is perfect for dipping roasted potatoes or other vegetables, but it's also perfect for a pasta salad dressing, a sandwich spread, or a potato salad.

Makes about 2 cups

2 dried aji amarillo chile peppers or 2 tablespoons aji amarillo powder

2 cups dairy or vegan mayonnaise

2 tablespoons fresh lemon juice, from about 1 lemon (squeeze the rest into a glass of water to drink)

sea salt and pepper

1. If using the dried aji amarillo chile peppers, place them into a bowl of boiling water and let them set for about 15 minutes until they soften.

2. Drain the aji amarillo peppers and remove and discard the stems. Using a sharp paring knife, slit open the peppers and scrape out the seeds, either with a small spoon or your fingers. Wash your hands after handling the hot peppers. Pat the peppers dry.

3. Place the drained peppers into the bowl of a food processor fitted with a metal blade. Add the mayonnaise, lemon juice, and a little salt and pepper. Cover and process for about 1 minute until smooth and well blended, stopping once to scrape down the sides of the processor bowl using a rubber spatula. Taste for seasoning. Turn into a bowl, using a rubber spatula to scrape all the delicious contents of the processor bowl.

4. If you are using the dried aji amarillo powder, just measure all the ingredients into a bowl and whisk together until blended. Taste for seasoning.

5. Cover and refrigerate for up to two weeks before using.

entrées, pastas, and entrée sandwiches

We've all been there—that time of the day when we're wondering what we can make for dinner. And if you prepare dinner often, the challenge is downright frightening! My neighbor Fred, who cooks for himself and his dad mostly every night, sometimes stops over to ask, "What should I make for dinner tonight?" and I try to offer suggestions.

Below are some of the suggestions I offer him. Sandwiches have really taken over in a lot of households at dinnertime. I know several friends who find that a sandwich with a salad is a delicious and easier way to get din-ner on the table on those work nights when time is short. The Arthur Avenue Sandwich is my favorite because I love broccoli rabe, but we have customers who say our Reuben Sandwich (page 100) is the best they've ever had. That's testimony enough for me! Mix it up. And please remember to add healthy vegetables to a couple of meals every single day, because that's the best way to achieve a delicious and healthier diet. Mix it up, but eat those vegetables! Seven to nine servings a day of fruits and vegetables is the way to go. You got this!

Pasta e' Ceci with Broccoli

One of the most frequently asked menu questions continues to be "What are your pasta dishes today?" We always offer our Pasta Marinara, and recently we've added our vegan Italian sausages to this entrée to add protein, making it a more complete meal. Our customers love it! We also make a pasta salad of the day, along with another one or two pasta dishes, and they always sell out. Everyone loves pasta.

For this dish I prefer ditalini (little tubes) or orecchiette (little ears) pasta, although a nice lemon fettuccine is yummy, too. If you need gluten-free, we often make gluten-free pasta dishes as well. I recommend Colavita and Garofalo brands of gluten-free pastas, but my all-time favorite gluten-free pasta is Le Veneziane. It's tender and flavorful, and honestly, it's perfect for an everyday pasta because it's that good! We use dry beans at Claire's because we have the time it takes to cook them, but at home, as we all know, we need to save time when we can, so I often use canned organic chickpeas. I love to add broccoli to this dish, which adds both flavor and health benefits from this vitamin, mineral, fiber-rich cruciferous vegetable.

Serves 6

1 pound pasta of choice

salt

1 8–10 ounce bag organic broccoli florets

½ cup extra-virgin olive oil, plus additional for drizzling over pasta/broccoli

8 cloves garlic, sliced

1 large shallot, finely chopped

3 ribs organic celery, sliced thin

1 small yellow onion, cut in half then thinly sliced

1 small bunch Italian flat-leaf parsley, finely chopped

½ teaspoon crushed red pepper flakes

1 teaspoon dried oregano

1 small bunch basil, leaves and tender stems coarsely chopped

1 bay leaf

salt and pepper

2 15.5-ounce cans organic chickpeas, drained

3 tablespoons freshly squeezed lemon juice, from about 1 lemon

1. Bring a large pot of salted water to a boil over high heat. Cook the pasta according to package directions. Add the broccoli florets during the last minute of cooking. Remove and set aside 6 cups of the pasta liquid before draining. Drain the pasta and turn into a large bowl. Drizzle lightly with olive oil and, using two spoons, toss to coat.

2. Heat the olive oil in a large pot over low-medium heat. Add the garlic, shallot, celery, onion, parsley, red pepper flakes, oregano, basil, bay leaf, and salt and pepper. Cover and cook for about 20 minutes, stirring frequently until the vegetables are barely tender. Add the chickpeas and the 6 cups of reserved cooking water. Cover and raise the heat to high and bring to a boil. Lower the heat to low-medium and simmer, stirring frequently, for about 15 minutes, until the sauce has reduced a little. Taste for seasoning. Using a potato masher, mash the chickpeas slightly. Add the lemon juice and stir to combine. Add the cooked pasta and broccoli. Using two spoons, toss well to coat. Turn into a large serving bowl. Drizzle a little extra olive oil evenly over the top.

3. Refrigerate any leftovers for lunch the next day.

Peperonata Sauce

Many years ago, I met the sister-in-law of the caterer for a party I was attending, and of course, we talked about food! She told me about this sauce that her mom made in Bari, Italy, when she was young. I was intrigued because, for one thing, I love organic red and yellow bell peppers, and I also love all tomato sauces. But this sauce had an ingredient I wouldn't have thought to use in a tomato sauce—cloves! As she described the sauce, in her magnificent Italian accent, I made notes. Well, it's been a hit at Claire's since that very next day when I tried to make it based on my notes. The cloves add an interesting flavor. That, and the more expected oregano and basil. I hope you'll try it.

Makes enough for a pound of pasta (I like a wet pasta)

1 35-ounce can whole peeled San Marzano tomatoes in juice

½ cup water

½ cup extra-virgin olive oil

2 medium yellow onions, finely chopped

6 cloves garlic, cut into medium slices

2 large organic bell peppers, two red, or one red and one orange or yellow, seeded and cut into a coarse chop

salt and pepper to taste

10 large basil leaves

1 small bunch Italian flat-leaf parsley, well washed and coarsely chopped

2 bay leaves

1 tablespoon dried oregano

½ teaspoon ground cloves

a shake or two of cayenne pepper

1. Turn the canned tomatoes into a bowl. Using your hands or a potato masher, squeeze the tomatoes to crush. Measure the ½ cup of water into the empty can of tomatoes, swish it around and add this to the tomatoes. Good tomatoes are too good to waste even a drop. Set aside.

2. Heat the oil in an 8-quart pot over medium heat. Add the onion, garlic, and peppers. Sprinkle with a little salt and pepper. Stir to combine. Cover and cook for about 10 minutes, stirring occasionally, until the vegetables have softened.

3. Stir in the tomatoes and the water, the basil leaves, parsley, bay leaves, oregano, cloves, and cayenne pepper. Cover and raise the heat to high and bring to a boil; then reduce the heat to low, cover, and continue cooking at a low boil, stirring frequently, for about 20 minutes, until the sauce is rich and slightly reduced.

4. Taste for seasoning. Spoon over your favorite pasta and toss to coat. I love this sauce with rigatoni or paccheri cooked al dente.

Arthur Avenue Sandwich

Entrée sandwiches have become such a popular post-pandemic supper, and we're not exactly sure why, but we do love a good sandwich! We make this popular sandwich with sauteed, garlicky broccoli rabe and tomatoes, which are piled over a grilled split sausage link, with or without shredded mozzarella on top—all on a baguette or a good Italian bread loaf. We sell many of these sandwiches for dinner. Broccoli rabe is loaded with vitamins A and C and potassium—all important nutrients for better vision and better immunity. And studies have shown that the lycopene in tomatoes reduces the chances of prostate cancer. Let's help our boys and men to a deliciously healthy sandwich. There are so many protein-rich and delicious vegan sausages today, so try a few and find your favorites. We use Tofurky vegan Italian sausages at Claire's Corner Copia.

This recipe makes enough for four sandwiches, but if you're cooking for one or two, don't let that stop you. Just cook the broccoli rabe and save any that you don't use. Leftover broccoli rabe is wonderful tossed with pasta (I love it with orecchiette—little ears) or just enjoy it as a side dish with your next supper.

Makes 4 sandwiches

¼ cup extra-virgin olive oil

4 cloves garlic, sliced into thin slices

1 large organic tomato, coarsely chopped, with juices

⅛ teaspoon red pepper flakes

¼ teaspoon fennel seeds

salt and pepper to taste

1 large bunch broccoli rabe, ¼ inch from stem cut off and discarded, and remaining cut into 1-inch pieces, well washed and drained

olive oil spray

4 links vegan Italian sausages, sliced to split in half lengthwise

4 small baguettes, about 7 inches each, cut open lengthwise for sandwiches (don't cut all the way through)

4 ounces shredded mozzarella, dairy or vegan (optional)

1. Heat the olive oil in a heavy pot over medium heat. Add the garlic and cook, stirring frequently for 1 minute until lightly browned, but don't let it burn. Add the tomato with the juices, red pepper flakes, fennel seeds, and a little salt and pepper. Cook, stirring frequently, for about 2 minutes until the tomatoes are softened. Add the drained broccoli rabe and sprinkle with salt and pepper. Using tongs, turn the broccoli rabe to coat with the oil. Cook for about 5 minutes, until tender to your preference, using tongs to occasionally turn the broccoli rabe. Taste for seasonings. Set aside while you heat your sausage links.

2. Spray a grill pan with olive oil spray and set over high heat. Add the sausage links, cut side down. Cook for about 30 seconds, and, using tongs, turn to heat the other side—they're already cooked so you're just heating them. Using a big spoon (you don't want to waste the yummy juices), arrange a quarter of the cooked broccoli rabe onto each baguette, then add one link (two halves), and top with about ¼ cup shredded mozzarella if desired.

Grilled Cheese Sandwich

Grilled Cheese Sandwiches are having their time in the sun again! Our customers, kiddos and adults, have fallen back in love with these creamy sandwiches, and honestly, they are so very delicious, satisfying, and filling, with or without Cream of Tomato Soup (page 77). You can make them with dairy or vegan cheeses. Again, we have fans on both sides, so we offer both.

Serve them for lunch alone or with a small salad or a vegetable and bean soup, and for dinner we suggest you add a big salad with organic romaine, tomatoes, red onions, carrots, beets, and other veggies, because, after all, we want people to eat seven to nine servings of fruits and vegetables every day, so every meal counts toward that healthy goal. You can embellish these cheese-filled pockets of love with sliced organic tomatoes, smoked tempeh bacon, sliced ripe avocado, sliced red onions, or roasted peppers, although straight up Grilled Cheese Sandwiches are fan favorites at our place. They are pretty decadent, so it would be a good idea to go easy on the calories for your other meals for the day. No judgment, just saying . . .

Makes 1 sandwich

2 slices good multigrain bread

2 tablespoons mayonnaise, dairy or vegan

olive oil spray

½ cup shredded mozzarella or cheddar, or a combination, dairy or vegan

1. Preheat the oven to 400 degrees. Spread both sides of each slice of bread with the mayonnaise, about ½ tablespoon per side of each slice of bread.

2. Heat a cast iron grill pan over medium heat until hot. Spray the pan with olive oil spray. Place the slices of bread, single layer onto the hot grill pan. Leave it untouched for about 1 minute, or until the underside has golden, medium brown grill marks when carefully lifted to check with a metal spatula. Using the spatula, carefully turn the slices of bread over to cook the other side for about 30 seconds. Sprinkle one slice of the bread with the shredded cheese. Using the spatula, flip the bare slice over onto the bread with the cheese. Gently press the sandwich together with the spatula.

3. Carefully transfer the hot grill pan to the oven. Bake for about 3 minutes until the cheese is melted. Carefully remove the sandwiches to a cutting board and cut each in half crosswise. Enjoy!

Reuben Sandwich

Like the Grilled Cheese Sandwich, the Reuben Sandwich has made a return to our menu. We love that we can make a delicious vegetarian version of this quintessential deli sandwich. And with the delicious vegan cheeses and mayonnaises available, we can also make this satisfying sandwich vegan. You can, too. We make our own Sauerkraut and Russian Dressing (page 101), but if you are in a pinch, you can always use store-bought for a quick sandwich. Our pasta salad, potato salad, and cole slaw are popular sides to serve with this sandwich, but a nice organic arugula salad would be great, too. Enjoy this super delicious, messy affair!

Makes 1 sandwich

2 slices good rye bread

olive oil spray

4 strips smoked tempeh bacon, or other vegetarian smoked bacon (we use Light Life)

¼ cup shredded Swiss cheese, dairy or vegan

2 slices organic beefsteak tomato

1 slice red onion

⅓ cup sauerkraut, homemade or store-bought

2 tablespoons Russian dressing, homemade or store-bought

1. Preheat the oven to 400 degrees. Lightly toast the rye bread. Place the toast, single layer, onto a cookie sheet lined with parchment paper for easy clean up. Set aside.

2. Heat a small skillet over high heat. Spray the skillet with olive oil spray. Carefully arrange the tempeh bacon strips single layer onto the hot skillet. Cook for about 30 seconds, until the underside is lightly browned when lifted with a metal spatula. Turn the bacon strips over and brown the other side for about 15 seconds.

3. Start building your sandwich. Transfer the cooked bacon to one side of the toasted rye bread. Add the shredded Swiss cheese over the bacon. Top with tomato slices, the onion, and the sauerkraut. Spoon the Russian dressing over the top. Carefully place the remaining slice of rye toast on top. Gently press the sandwich together.

4. Bake in the preheated oven for 5 minutes, until the cheese is melted. Enjoy it!

Sauerkraut

Sauerkraut is so versatile! Serve it on the side of any sandwich and you are transported to your favorite deli, especially if you are adding it to your Reuben. I like sauerkraut so much that I sometimes eat it with a good mustard and pickle relish as a side to just about any sandwich. If you haven't already tried it on a baguette with a grilled vegan sausage link and your favorite mustard, you are in for a treat! Yes, I'm obsessed with sauerkraut! And it's so easy to make. I do hope you'll make a batch and enjoy it many delicious ways.

Makes about 7 cups

1 large head green cabbage, cored and thinly sliced

6 cups white vinegar

4 cups water

½ cup salt

1. Put all the ingredients into a heavy pot. Stir well to combine. Cover and bring to a boil over high heat. Once it reaches a boil, remove the cover, lower the heat to medium, and cook at a low-medium boil for about 10 minutes, stirring occasionally, until the cabbage is fully wilted.

2. Drain and turn onto a cookie sheet to cool to room temperature. Once it's cooled to room temperature, turn into a jar, label, and store in the refrigerator for up to two weeks.

Russian Dressing

Everything old seems to be new again! Russian dressing was "a thing" back when we first opened in 1975, then its popularity slowed down. But wait. It's back! And it really is a delicious dressing for a green tossed salad or a potato or pasta salad, and absolutely for a Reuben Sandwich, which by the way, is also having its moment again.

Makes 1½ cups

1 cup vegan mayonnaise

¼ cup ketchup

1 large dill pickle, sliced

2 tablespoons pickle juice

salt and pepper

1. Measure the ingredients into a blender cup. Cover and blend on high speed for about a minute, until the mixture is well blended. Taste for seasonings.

2. Store in a jar in the fridge for up to two weeks. Be sure to label and date your jar.

Buffalo Tofu Wings

These wings are addictive! We serve these plant-based wings with our Creamy Vegan Potato Salad (page 79) over organic arugula and they are very popular. Great for dinner and also perfect for your next Super Bowl Party!

Makes 8 wings, serves 4

1 16-ounce refrigerated, water-packed container super firm organic tofu (I love Nasoya brand)

1 cup cornstarch

salt and pepper

1 cup Frank's Hot Sauce

¼ cup vegan butter

2 cups GMO-free canola oil

1. Line a cookie sheet with a triple layer of paper towels. Drain the container of tofu, cut the block in half lengthwise, then cut each half into four log-shaped (wings) sticks. Set onto the paper towel–lined cookie sheet, leaving a little space in between each wing. Top with another triple layer of paper towels and top with another cookie sheet. Using your hands, press the top pan onto the bottom sheet to squeeze out excess water. Don't press too hard or you'll crush the wings. If you don't have a second cookie sheet, just use your hands to press gently onto the wings to remove some of the excess water. This helps the cornstarch stick better.

2. Measure the cornstarch into a glass pie plate large enough to hold about four of the wings. Sprinkle the cornstarch with salt and pepper, then whisk gently to combine. Set aside.

3. Measure the hot sauce and the vegan butter into a medium pot (big enough to dip the wings into, a few at a time) and heat this over medium heat, stirring occasionally, until the vegan butter melts and the mixture is warm. Remove the pan from the stove and set on a trivet on the counter by the stove.

4. Measure the oil into a deep skillet over medium-high heat on a back burner—it's always safer to fry on a back burner. Set another sheet pan with either a drain rack over it or line it with parchment paper and set by the stove for the fried wings. Set a plate by the bowl of seasoned cornstarch. Have a set of long tongs ready to turn your wings. Add a few tofu wings to the seasoned cornstarch, then shake off excess and place on the plate.

5. Heat the oil until it sizzles when you dip a tofu wing into it. Arrange the wings, single layer, into the hot oil and let them cook for about 1 minute, until they are a pale golden color. Turn to cook all sides, about 1 more minute. Transfer to the drain rack or parchment paper–lined cookie sheet. Work quickly and dredge a few more wings into the seasoned cornstarch while the wings are frying so you'll be ready when the others are cooked. Continue dredging, frying, and draining the wings. Then, using the tongs, dip each wing into the hot sauce/vegan butter mix, then return to the drain rack. Dip each tofu wing into the hot sauce/vegan butter mix a second time. Place the fried and dipped wings onto the drain rack or the lined cookie sheet. Serve with Creamy Vegan Potato Salad (page 79).

Blackened Oyster Mushroom Tacos

These are our most popular tacos at Claire's Corner Copia, and we prepare them with the best local and organic oyster mushrooms. These gorgeous and meaty mushrooms are dusted with a spicy pan-blackening seasoning, and the fact that they are fried crispy, using GMO-free canola oil (we use the oil only once for freshness), makes them super delicious.

Oyster mushrooms are sold in clusters, so you'll want to separate the clusters into individual mushrooms so they'll fit on the tortillas.

Serves 4

4 heaping cups oyster mushrooms

1½ cups cornstarch

½ cup pan-blackening seasoning

3 cups GMO-free canola oil

8 organic corn tortillas

1. Separate the clusters of mushrooms into individual mushrooms. Rinse the mushrooms, then drain well. Put a triple layer of paper towels onto a cookie sheet; then, using your fingers, carefully tear any really large mushrooms into two. Scatter the mushrooms, single layer, onto the paper-lined cookie sheet. Top with a layer of paper towels and gently press to dry the mushrooms. Set aside while you proceed with the recipe.

2. Preheat the oven to 400 degrees. Set a cookie sheet with a drain rack, or lined with a triple layer of paper towels, by the stove. Have long-handled tongs by the stove. Measure the cornstarch into a medium bowl and measure the blackening seasoning into another medium bowl.

3. Heat the canola oil in a medium pot over high heat—on the back burner (it's safer to always fry on a back burner).

4. Add the drained oyster mushrooms to the bowl of cornstarch, and, using two spoons, toss to coat. You'll want to work fast. One by one, lift a mushroom out of the cornstarch, shake off the excess cornstarch, and set onto the cookie sheet with the drain rack. They should fit on one half of the cookie sheet, leaving the other half for the fried mushrooms. Test the oil for heat. It should sizzle when you dip a cornstarch-coated mushroom into it. Once it's hot enough to fry the mushrooms, add three or four mushrooms. Don't crowd the pot or the mushrooms will be soggy and not crispy. Fry the mushrooms for about 2 minutes, using your tongs to turn the mushrooms after 1 minute, until all sides are

lightly browned. Using your tongs, carefully remove the cooked mushrooms to the drain rack. Continue frying the remaining mushrooms. Once the mushrooms are fried, turn off the heat and allow the oil to cool before removing it from the stove. It's too dangerous to ever move a pot of hot oil. Transfer a few of the fried mushrooms to the bowl of blackening seasoning and toss well to coat, using two spoons. Return to the drain rack and continue tossing the remaining fried mushrooms.

5. Arrange the corn tortillas onto a parchment-lined cookie sheet and heat in the preheated oven for about 2 minutes, until warmed. Arrange them, single layer, onto a platter. Top each with a few of the blackened mushrooms, Cabbage and Pineapple Cole Slaw (page 108), and Pickled Red Onions, Carrots, and Jalapeños (page 107), or your favorite toppings. Serve with Refried Beans (page 129) and Salsa (page 131) or your favorite side dishes.

Pickled Red Onions, Carrots, and Jalapeños

We make this traditional and delicious topping for our tacos, but we make plenty extra for our salads—it adds an interesting sweet, pickled heat to green salads, sandwiches, and veggie burgers.

Makes enough for tacos and to top your dinner salad

1½ large red onions, peeled, cut in half, sliced into thin ribs, separated

1 medium carrot, thinly sliced

1 jalapeño pepper, seeded and thinly sliced (be sure to wash your hands after handling hot peppers before touching your face or you'll feel the burn!)

¾ cup sugar

2 cups red wine vinegar

Put the onions, carrots, and jalapeño peppers into a medium bowl. Scatter the sugar evenly over the top and using two spoons, toss to coat. Pour the vinegar evenly over the top, and using two spoons, toss well to coat. You can enjoy them immediately, but we usually let them marinate for 1–2 hours, but enjoy them for up to four days and they'll soften and continue to treat your tastebuds.

Cabbage and Pineapple Cole Slaw

We love cabbage salads (cole slaw) at Claire's! We make all sorts of cole slaws and serve them on top of our tacos or as a side salad with our sandwiches. Some of our customers even order this cole slaw as their main salad. This slaw has chunks of pineapple and cilantro, which adds to the freshness of this delicious salad, with a nice kick of heat from the jalapeño. Serve this wonderful cole slaw at your next cookout. I also love this slaw with grilled vegan Italian sausages on a hot dog bun.

Serves 4–6

1 large head Savoy cabbage, cut in half, cored, and sliced thin

1 ounce bunch cilantro, rinsed and minced

1 jalapeño, seeded and minced (wash your hands after handling hot peppers or you will burn your eyes or face if you touch them)

1¼ cup vegan mayonnaise

salt and pepper

2 cups fresh pineapple chunks, finely chopped, include the juices

½ small red onion, peeled, cut in half and finely chopped

Put the sliced cabbage into a big bowl. Scatter the minced cilantro and minced jalapeño pepper evenly over the cabbage. Add the remaining ingredients. Using two spoons, toss the slaw to combine the ingredients. Taste for seasonings.

oldies but goodies (aka the most loved of all our menu items)

This chapter holds the most favorite recipes we make! Really, they are the foundation of our success. So much so that they've remained on our menu for decades, and we cannot imagine ever taking them off. I hope you'll love them, too, and find that you pass them down to your friends and family, and to your children's children.

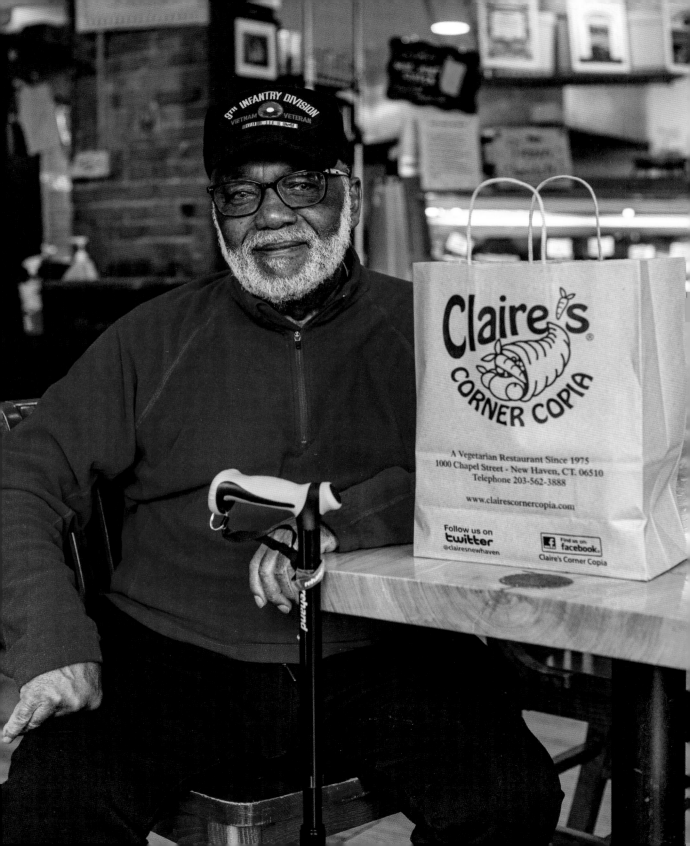

Lithuanian Coffee Cake

Generally, when you ask anyone who knows our sweet little place, the first thing they say is "Try the Lithuanian Coffee Cake," and we love that! It's our signature cake.

People always ask how this recipe and the name come about. Back in the early days, a great gal, Sally Tessler, worked with us. One day she brought in her mom's recipe for a coffee cake. I'm Italian American, and in our family, we eat biscotti with our coffee or espresso, so basically, a coffee cake to me meant coffee in a cake. Who knew? The original recipe didn't have coffee, so I altered the recipe to add it, but I didn't want to offend Sally or her mom, so I didn't mention it. Well, Sally loved the cake! We called the cake Sally Tessler's Mother's Coffee Cake, which was quite a long name, so after a while, I asked her where the recipe came from, and Sally said, "It was my grandmother's recipe and she's from what was Lithuania, but now it's part of the Soviet bloc." Well, we decided to Bring Back Lithuania. We made signs for our windows that read: "Just Say Lithuania!" and "Lithuanian Coffee Cake!" When Lithuania once again became an independent country, Sally called to ask if our signs might have helped. I wish it could be that easy. I hope you will love this cake like we do.

Serves 10–12

FILLING

¼ cup packed dark brown sugar

2 tablespoons granulated sugar

1 teaspoon cinnamon

1 tablespoon ground coffee (not brewed)

¼ cup chopped walnuts

¼ cup raisins

CAKE

8 tablespoons (1 stick) butter, softened to room temperature

1 cup granulated sugar

2 eggs

1 tablespoon brewed coffee, chilled

1 teaspoon pure vanilla extract

1 cup sour cream (we use full fat for creaminess)

2 cups unbleached flour

1 teaspoon baking soda

1 teaspoon baking powder

Nonstick baking spray

Powdered sugar, glaze, or buttercream frosting for topping (optional)

Claire's CORNER COPIA

Our Signature
Lithuanian
Coffee Cake
Contains Walnuts

1. Prepare the filling by combining the ingredients in a small bowl. Stir well to combine. Set aside. Preheat the oven to 350 degrees.

2. For the cake, cream the butter and sugar in a mixing bowl using a hand mixer on medium speed for 45 seconds. Scrape the sides down with a rubber spatula. Add the eggs and beat for 30 seconds. Scrape down the sides of the bowl. Add the coffee, vanilla extract, and sour cream. Beat on low speed for 30 seconds, until well creamed. Scrape down the sides of the bowl.

3. In a separate bowl, sift the flour, baking soda, and baking powder. Pour the creamed mixture over the top of the flour mixture, scraping the bowl well. Mix on low speed for 45 seconds just to combine, stopping to scrape down the sides of the bowl.

4. Prepare a 10-cup bundt pan by thoroughly spraying with nonstick baking spray or greasing with shortening and flouring the pan. Pour in half the batter. Sprinkle half the filling evenly over the top of the batter. Pour the remaining batter evenly over the filling. Use a rubber spatula to scrape the batter from the bowl and to smooth the batter. Sprinkle the remaining filling evenly over the batter.

5. Bake in the center of the oven for 50–55 minutes, until a cake tester inserted into the center comes out clean. Remove the cake from the oven and let it cool in the pan for 5 minutes, then turn it out onto a plate. Serve warm or cooled to room temperature, dusted with powdered sugar, drizzled with glaze, or frosted with Buttercream Frosting (page 123).

Carrot Cake

This is the second most popular cake at Claire's Corner Copia, nearly fifty years later! The recipe came from my Aunt Jerry, one of the best bakers I've ever known. Many years ago, I was a little surprised to see carrots in her cake, but one bite was all I needed to be a fan. This cake is so moist with pineapple and walnuts and is delicious served alone, but top with our Buttercream Frosting (page 123) and it becomes a really special treat. Over the years, we've received poems and even an ode to this cake, and honestly, it's that good! I hope it becomes a big hit in your family, too.

Serves 8–10

1½ cups unbleached flour

1½ cups sugar

1 teaspoon salt

2 teaspoons baking soda

2 teaspoons cinnamon

½ teaspoon ground nutmeg

3 eggs

¾ cup GMO-free canola oil

1 cup drained crushed pineapple

¾ cup grated carrots

¾ cup chopped walnuts

⅓ cup raisins

Nonstick baking spray

1. Preheat oven to 350 degrees. In a large bowl, whisk together the flour, sugar, salt, baking soda, cinnamon, and nutmeg. In a separate bowl, beat the eggs for 1 minute, using a hand mixer on low speed. Add the oil and mix on medium speed for 1 minute. Stir in the drained pineapple. Pour this mixture all at once over the dry ingredients and stir to mix lightly to combine. Stir in the carrots, walnuts, and raisins. Mix just to combine, using a spoon.

2. Prepare a 10-cup bundt pan with nonstick baking spray, or grease and flour the pan. Pour the batter into the prepared pan, using a rubber spatula to scrape the bowl clean and to smooth the top. Bake in the center of the oven for about 1 hour and 10 minutes, or until a cake tester inserted into the center comes out clean. Remove from the oven and let stand for 5 minutes, then turn out onto a plate and cool to room temperature before frosting with Buttercream Frosting (page 123).

Buttercream Frosting

This Buttercream Frosting has frosted literally thousands of cakes and whoopie pies, and many athletic teams at Yale University have ordered dozens of "frosting shots" for pregame meets. I guess what I'm saying is that this buttercream is a winner! Enjoy every buttery spoonful.

Makes enough to frost 1 bundt cake

4 tablespoons (½ stick) butter, at room temperature

4 tablespoons trans fat–free margarine (we use organic Earth Balance), at room temperature

2 cups confectioners' sugar, sifted

1 teaspoon pure vanilla extract

Using a hand mixer on medium speed, beat together the butter and margarine for about 3 minutes or until light and creamy. Scrape down the sides of the bowl with a rubber spatula as needed. Add the confectioners' sugar, ½ cup at a time, beating about 2 minutes after each addition, until light and creamy. Beat in the vanilla extract.

Marinara Sauce

Marinara is the perfect sauce for any pasta, eggplant parmesan, and lasagne, and as a sauce for filled breads. Our Marinara Sauce has been on our menu from day one, and it remains our favorite kitchen staple. Make a double batch and freeze half for those emergency suppers when you just don't know what to make. I like to keep spinach and ricotta ravioli in my freezer, and with this sauce a delicious dinner is on the table without a lot of effort. Just make a beautiful salad and you're ready for an easy and delicious night.

Makes about 5 cups, perfect for a pound of pasta (I like my pasta well sauced)

¼ cup extra-virgin olive oil

6 large cloves garlic, cut into thick slices

2 shallots, coarsely chopped

1 35-ounce can whole peeled San Marzano tomatoes in juice, squeezed with your hands to crush

½ cup red wine

10 large basil leaves

¼ cup finely chopped Italian flat-leaf parsley

2 bay leaves

salt and pepper

Heat the oil in a large pot over medium heat. Add the garlic and shallots. Cover and cook, stirring occasionally, for 7–10 minutes, or until the garlic and shallots are light brown but not burned. Add the remaining ingredients and stir well to mix. Cover and cook at a medium boil (this should take about 5 minutes), stirring occasionally, for about 20 minutes or until the sauce reduces slightly. Taste for seasonings.

Lentil Soup

Lentil soup is loaded with vitamins, minerals, protein, and fiber. It has been on our weekly rotation of soups since we opened—it's that good! Pair this yummy soup with a colorful salad for a terrific supper. This soup freezes well, too; just remember to label and date it.

Serves 8

4 quarts water

1 pound lentils, picked over

1 bay leaf

5 tablespoons extra-virgin olive oil

4 large garlic cloves, finely chopped

1 medium yellow onion, finely chopped

8 ribs celery, cut into ½-inch thick slices, including leaves

6 medium carrots, cut into ½-inch thick slices

1 medium fennel bulb, cut into bite-size pieces

1 6-ounce can tomato paste

¼ cup finely chopped Italian flat-leaf parsley

salt and pepper

1 10-ounce bag organic spinach, well washed and drained

2 cups tubetti pasta, cooked according to package directions

1. Place the water, lentils, and bay leaf in a large pot. Cover and bring to a boil over high heat. Lower the heat to medium. Add the oil, garlic, onion, celery, carrots, fennel, tomato paste, parsley, and a little salt and pepper. Stir well to mix. Cover and cook at a medium-high boil (the soup will return to a boil after about 5 minutes), stirring occasionally, for about 1 hour or until the lentils and celery are tender-soft.

2. Add the spinach. Stir well to mix. Cover and continue cooking, stirring occasionally, for 5 minutes, until the spinach is tender.

3. Stir in the cooked pasta. Taste for seasonings.

Split Pea Soup

Like our Lentil Soup, Split Pea Soup is a perennial favorite at Claire's Corner Copia! We couldn't be happier because it's super healthy—it's a delicious bowl of protein, fiber, vitamins, and minerals. This version also has vegan hot dogs added to it for a nice "meaty" flavor. Field Roast makes my favorite vegan hot dog, but try a few and choose one you like.

Serves 6

¼ cup extra-virgin olive oil

1 large sweet onion, coarsely chopped

3 large cloves garlic, coarsely chopped

6 medium carrots, cut into bite-size pieces

6 ribs celery, cut into bite-size pieces, including leaves

½ cup coarsely chopped Italian flat-leaf parsley

10 fresh basil leaves

salt and pepper to taste

3 quarts water

1 pound split peas, picked over

2 bay leaves

1 head escarole (about 1¼ pounds), well washed, cut into 2-inch pieces

1 14- to 16-ounce package meatless hot dogs, cut into ½-inch slices

1. Heat the oil in a large, heavy pot over medium-low heat. Add the onion, garlic, carrots, celery, parsley, basil, just a little salt (the hot dogs tend to be a little salty), and pepper. Stir to mix. Cover and cook for about 15 minutes, stirring occasionally until the vegetables have softened and released some of their moisture.

2. Add the water. Cover and raise the heat to high, bringing to a boil. Add the split peas, bay leaves, and escarole. Lower the heat to medium-low. Cover and cook, stirring occasionally, for about 1½ hours, or until the peas and vegetables are soft.

3. Add the meatless hot dogs. Cover and continue cooking for 4 minutes, stirring occasionally. Taste for seasonings.

French Peasant Soup

This is a hearty and savory stew-like soup, perfect any time of year but especially appreciated on chilly winter days and nights. All you need is slices of good Italian bread or a baguette, toasted and ready to dunk into this wonderful soup. Like many bean soups, this soup freezes well. My brother Paul makes a batch and brings containers to his daughters and to our niece. It's a terrific gift for a friend, too.

Serves 6

4 quarts water

12 ounces dry great northern beans, picked over

1 small yellow onion, coarsely chopped

8 cloves garlic, sliced thin

½ cup extra-virgin olive oil

¼ teaspoon dried thyme

1 bay leaf

¼ teaspoon dried basil

6 medium carrots, coarsely chopped

½ bunch celery, cut into ½-inch slices, including leaves

¼ cup finely chopped Italian flat-leaf parsley

4 tablespoons butter or Earth Balance vegan spread

1 small head green cabbage, cored and coarsely chopped

5 medium Yukon Gold potatoes, diced

salt and pepper

Bring the water to a boil in a large heavy pot. Add the beans and reduce the heat to medium. Cover and cook for 30 minutes, stirring frequently. Add the onion, garlic, olive oil, thyme, bay leaf, basil, carrots, celery, parsley, butter (or Earth Balance), and cabbage. Cover and bring to a boil. Reduce the heat to low and simmer for about 1½ hours, stirring frequently, until the beans are nearly tender. Add the potatoes and salt and pepper. Continue cooking, covered, at a low boil for about 30–45 minutes, until the beans are very soft and the soup is thick. Taste for seasoning.

Refried Beans AKA Refries

Refried beans are a main staple at Claire's—and have been from just about the very beginning of our story that started in 1975!

We have made Refries at Claire's for as long as I can remember, but we originally made them a little differently from this recipe. We had always used our cook Javier Lopez's recipe. He's from Mexico, so we always deferred to him for our Mexican recipes. One night, a bunch of us from Claire's went to my mom's for dinner. She made Refries as one of the side dishes, and all of us, including Javier, were totally impressed by how simple yet delicious these smooth and creamy beans were. This is my mom's recipe: Anna Pasqualina Bigio LaPia. We really do all get a seat at the proverbial table. And we're better for it! Serve these delicious and healthy, fiber- and protein-rich beans as a side to your Huevos Rancheros (page 27) or in a burrito, quesadilla, taco, or tostada—or on our Baja Plate. Sometimes, I just eat these beans with a little brown rice for lunch. It's comforting and delicious!

Serves 4–6 as a side

1 pound dry pinto beans, picked over for stones, rinsed and drained

1 bay leaf

⅓ cup extra-virgin olive oil

1 large onion, cut in half, then into thin slices

salt

1. Cook the beans according to the package directions, adding the bay leaf. Before draining, reserve 1 cup of the cooking liquid. (To help remember to reserve the cooking liquid, I like to place a measuring cup in the colander/strainer that I place in the sink for draining.)

2. Heat the olive oil in a large, deep skillet over low-medium heat. Add the onion slices and a little salt and stir to combine. Cover and cook for about 10 minutes, stirring frequently, until the onions are soft and golden. Add the drained beans and reserved cooking liquid to the onions in the skillet. Using a potato masher, mash the beans until smooth and creamy. Taste for seasonings.

Salsa

We make 20-plus quarts of our Salsa pretty much every day, and we serve it with chips and guacamole and many of our other Mexican dishes, including our ever-popular Huevos Rancheros (page 27). You might wonder why we don't put cilantro in our salsa. Well, three decades ago, when Rose Naclerio (Albin) was our fabulous manager, cilantro upset her during her pregnancies, even to smell, so we eliminated it from our recipe. Customers loved it and still do, so we never added it back in. This recipe makes a nice amount for a dip for your corn chips, for quesadillas and burritos, and for Huevos Rancheros.

Makes about 5 cups

1 35-ounce can whole peeled San Marzano tomatoes in juice, squeezed to crush with your hands

¼ cup extra-virgin olive oil

1 large yellow onion, cut in half, then cut into thin ribs

6 cloves garlic, sliced

1 small bunch Italian flat-leaf parsley, finely chopped

2 4-ounce cans peeled chopped green chile peppers

½ teaspoon crushed red pepper flakes

2 teaspoons chili powder

2 teaspoons ground cumin

2 teaspoons dried oregano

salt and black pepper

1 cup water

Combine all ingredients into a large heavy pot over high heat. Stir well to combine. Bring to a boil, stirring frequently, then lower the heat to medium. Cook at a low boil, stirring frequently, for about 30 minutes, until the sauce has cooked to your liking. Taste for seasonings. Use while hot, or turn onto a large deep pan to cool to room temperature before refrigerating.

The only compelling reason we've been given more love than we need, more food than we need, and more resources than we need, is so that we may share with others who have been given less - "God Squad"

recipe index